SEMEIA 27

Law as Literature

Editor of This Issue:
William Scott Green

Wipf & Stock
PUBLISHERS
Eugene, Oregon

Wipf and Stock Publishers
199 W 8th Ave, Suite 3
Eugene, OR 97401

Law as Literature
By Neusner, Jacob
Copyright©1983 by Neusner, Jacob
ISBN: 1-59752-063-2
Publication date 1/1/2006
Previously published by Scholars Press, 1983

CONTENTS

Contributors to this Issue	iv
Abbreviations	v
Transliterations	vii

INTRODUCTION
Law as Literature
  William Scott Green 1

FORM ANALYSIS AND EXEGESIS
The Case of Mishnah Tohorot 2:2–8
  Jacob Neusner 5

FORM AS MEANING IN HALAKIC *MIDRASH*
A Programmatic Statement
  Jack N. Lightstone 23

CONTEMPORARY EXEGESIS OF TALMUDIC LITERATURE
The Work of Shamma Friedman, David Weiss Halivni,
and Abraham Weiss

  I. Introduction: Metaphor and Exegesis
     Jacob Neusner 37

  II. The Work of Shamma Friedman

     i. Shamma Friedman's Methodological Principles
        David Weiner 45
     ii. Shamma Friedman on b. Yebamot 87b–88a
        Louis Newman 53
     iii. Shamma Friedman on b. Yebamot 88a-b
        Roger Brooks 63
     iv. Shamma Friedman on b. Yebamot 88b–89a
        Judith Romney Wegner 77

  III. The Work of David Weiss Halivni:
     A Source-Critical Commentary to b. Yebamot 87b
        Louis Newman 93

  IV. Abraham Weiss as Exegete and Text-Critic:
     The Case of b. Berakot 35b
        Roger Brooks and Joseph M. Davis 103

REDACTION AND FORMULATION
The Talmud of the Land of Israel and the Mishnah
  Jacob Neusner 117

CONTRIBUTORS TO THIS ISSUE

Roger Brooks
  Program in Judaic Studies
  Brown University
  Providence, RI 02912

Joseph M. Davis
  The Jewish Theological Seminary of America
  New York, NY 10027

Jack N. Lightstone
  Department of Religion
  Condordia University
  Montreal, Quebec, Canada H3G 1M8

Jacob Neusner
  Program in Judaic Studies
  Brown University
  Providence, RI 02912

Louis Newman
  Department of Religious Studies
  Carleton College
  Northfield, MN 55057

Judith Romney Wegner
  Program in Judaic Studies
  Brown University
  Providence, RI 02912

David Weiner
  Department of Philosophy
  Yale University
  New Haven, CT 06520

ABBREVIATIONS

b.	Babylonian Talmud
B.M.	Baba Meṣia
C	H. Loewe, The Mishnah of the Palestinian Talmud [Hebrew] (Jerusalem, 1967)
Chr.	Chronicles
Deut.	Deuteronomy
Ex.	Exodus
Gen.	Genesis
GRA	Elijah ben Solomon Zalman ("Elijah Gaon" or "Vilna Gaon"), 1720–1797. From Mishnah, ed. Romm (Vilna, 1887)
Hul.	Hullin
K	Georg Beer, *Faksimilie-Ausgabe des Mischnacodex Kaufmann A 50* (Reprint: Jerusalem, 1968)
Katsh	Abraham I. Katsh, *Ginze Mishnah. One Hundred and Forty-Nine Fragments from the Cairo Geniza in the Saltykov-Schedrin Library in Leningrad* (Jerusalem, 1970)
Ker.	Keritot
Lev.	Leviticus
M.	Mishnah
M	*Babylonian Talmud Codex Munich (95)* (reprint: Jerusalem, 1971)
MA	*Mishnah Aharonah*, Ephraim Isaac of Premsyla. Published in 1882; from reprint of Mishnah, ed. Romm
Maimonides text	*Mishnah ʿim Perush Rabbenu Moshe ben Maimon*. Trans. Joseph David Qappah. *VI Seder Tohorot* (Jerusalem, 1968)
N	*Mishnah ʿim Perush HaRambam. Defus Rishon Napoli [5]252 (1492)* (Jerusalem, 1970)
Neg.	Negaʿim
Neh.	Nehemiah
Num.	Numbers
P	*Shishah Sidré Mishnah. Ketav Yad Parma DeRossi 138* (Jerusalem, 1970)

Pa	*Mishnah Ketab Yad Paris 328–329* (reprint: Jerusalem, 1973)
PB	*Mishnah Codex Parma "B" DeRossi 497. Seder Tohorot Introduction by M. Bar Asher* (reprint: Jerusalem, 1971)
R.	Rabbi
Rosh	Asher ben Yehiel, ca. 1250-1327. From reprint of Mishnah Seder Tohorot in Babylonian Talmud, ed. Romm (Vilna, 1887)
Sam.	Samuel
San.	Sanhedrin
Shebu.	Shebuʿot
Sot.	Sotah
T.	Tosefta
Toh.	Tohorot
TYY	Tiferet Yisrael Yakhin. Israel ben Gedaliah Lipschutz, 1782–1860 (with supercommentary of Baruch Isaac Lipschutz), from reprint of Mishnah, ed. Romm
V	*Seder Tohorot ʿim Perush . . . Moshe bar Maimon. Nidpas ʿal yede Daniel Bomberg beshnat 5282 [= 1522]. Venezia* (Venice, 1522; reprint: Jerusalem, 1972).
y.	Palestinian Talmud
Yeb.	Yebamot

TRANSLITERATION OF HEBREW

א = ʾ
ב = b
ג = g
ד = d
ה = h
ו = w
ז = z
ח = ḥ
ט = ṭ
י = y
כ ך = k
ל = l
מ ם = m
נ ן = n
ס = s
ע = ʿ
פ ף = p
צ ץ = ṣ
ק = q
ר = r
שׁ = š
שׂ = ś
ת = t

INTRODUCTION: LAW AS LITERATURE

William Scott Green
The University of Rochester

Of all the cognate writings employed in biblical research, perhaps none is so often cited yet so seldom read as the literature of rabbinic Judaism. Rabbinic material has found its way into biblical studies largely through the media of elaborate scholarly summaries, condensations, and anthologies of rabbinic documents. But, however comprehensive they are or practical they seem, such selective presentations of a rich and complex literature inevitably deflect attention away from the texts themselves and the problems of their meaning and interpretation. When rabbinic data are used to help unravel some exegetical or historical peculiarity in the biblical text, isolated and decontextualized passages normally supply the needed assistance. Biblical scholars have little occasion to see rabbinic documents whole, to apprehend their structure and dynamic, or to explore their analytical difficulties and hermeneutical challenges. For many students of scripture, especially those trained in established methods, the content of rabbinic literature remains unfamiliar, its preoccupations unconventional, and its discourse alien.

This issue of *Semeia* contributes a modest corrective to these conditions. The essays that follow contain substantial, and therefore useful, segments from highly representative rabbinic texts: the Mishnah, the Mekilta deRabbi Ishmael, the Babylonian Talmud, and the Palestinian Talmud. Their aim in part is to allow readers who irregularly encounter rabbinic writings to follow these texts closely, to watch them work, as it were, from the inside. But if this Issue were merely another collection, an additional sampler of rabbinic snippets, it hardly could claim much attention. Rather, the essays gathered here also illustrate and evaluate the methods currently used in the study of rabbinic literature. Collectively they make a clear and forceful statement about the way rabbinic texts are to be read, analyzed, and understood. They signal the emergence in rabbinic scholarship of the text as an object of study in its own right.

As most readers of this journal doubtless know, rabbinic literature treats two broad subjects: *halakah* (rabbinic praxis) and the interpretation of scripture. Though rabbinic documents are dated from the third century through early medieval times, some materials in them allege to derive from the period of the second Temple. The documents offer few sustained essays. Rather, they are made up almost entirely of distinct and usually self-contained passages—sometimes brief halakic or exegetical sayings, sometimes more elaborated halakic discussions, sometimes narratives about rabbis or biblical figures—grouped neither biographically nor chronologically but in patterns of thematic, topical, or scriptural arrangement. Although they contain stories, rulings, and exegeses attributed to many rabbis, all rabbinic documents are anonymous and comprise substantial amounts of unassigned material. The mix of anonymity and collectivity in rabbinic writings is one of its most distinctive traits.

Scholars of rabbinism have used its literature primarily to write history or theology, and they consequently have construed rabbinic texts to be sources of rabbinic culture and religion, indefectible representations of society and politics, behavior and belief. Perhaps seduced by the documents' synchronicity, they have treated all rabbinic writings as a single, seamless composition and have read through or beyond the texts to uncover the historical reality or theological truth that allegedly lies behind them. This method makes the text into a vehicle to somewhere else, and the text itself becomes an epiphenomenon, a reflection, or a transparency. It thus is understandable that most studies of rabbinic theology are merely thematic catalogues, and most histories of rabbinism essentially chronologies, of discrete and decontextualized sayings, stories, and rulings.

Recent developments in hermeneutics, literary criticism, and the form-analysis of rabbinic literature have theoretically and practically challenged this method and forced a radical rethinking of its basic suppositions. It now seems naive and even willful to cling to the notion of a transparent text with a univocal meaning just below its surface. It now seems unwarranted to ignore the status of texts as products and cultural constructions, as data rather than sources. And it now is empirically impossible to affirm the homogeneity of all rabbinic writings. These arguments and insights, or versions of them, have slowed the rush to the backside of the text and have reshaped and redirected the study of rabbinic literature. In contemporary rabbinic studies the text itself is the primary object of interest, and scholars increasingly are aware that the foundation for all other inferences from a rabbinic text is a precise understanding of its construction.

The effect of this shift in scholarly interest is perhaps most evident and consequential in the study of rabbinic *halakah*. Because of its focus on particular actions in concrete situations, *halakah* usually is assumed to be, and normally is rendered into English as, law. Probably on account of its concern with behavior, scholars have tended to regard the halakic content of rabbinic texts as the most historically reliable, socially representative, and culturally revealing material in the literature. But, that halakic discourse inherently points beyond itself to describe Jewish communal life as lived in rabbinic antiquity is no certainty. Indeed, the traits of the literature make such a proposition less than self-evident.

Rabbinic literature in general is highly technical. Its halakic content in particular presupposes both considerable information and codes for interpretation. Even the most elementary halakic statement presumes a tacit dimension of rabbinic knowledge, attitudes, behaviors, and motivations. The terse and formulaic syntax of halakic discourse and its specialized vocabulary constitute a scholastic shorthand. Halakic discourse is directed to those already proficient in it and shields itself from the penetration of outsiders.

In sharp contrast to the medieval Jewish law codes, which were fashioned when rabbis dominated communal life, halakic discourse is filled with contention. In rabbinic documents rabbis routinely appear in disagreement with one another. But, especially in the earlier documents, these disputes tend to remain unresolved. The literary strategy of juxtaposing opposites without resolution blocks any perception of the social meaning of ideas and makes the social effect of dissent impossible to assess. It also wholly obscures internal social and political relationships of power and domination, and thus makes it difficult to discern who adopted, or was forced to adopt, a particular halakic practice.

Rabbinic literature contains countless examples of discussions of actions that were impossible to perform. More than half of the Mishnah and Tosefta is devoted to matters pertaining to the Temple cult, yet the documents were compiled and promulgated more than a century after the Temple's demise. Likewise, despite their concreteness, many halakic discussions in later documents are undeniably theoretical.

These traits admittedly do not confirm that rabbinic *halakah* did not direct and inform Jewish social life in antiquity, nor do they show that halakic discourse has no practical urgency. But they also do not demonstrate the contrary. That rabbinic literature, and *halakah* in particular, is inherently mimetic, a straightforward reflection of "what actually happened" in rabbinic antiquity, is thus no axiom. Indeed, the structure and form of rabbinic writings suggests that our first reading of these documents must see them not as records of collective behavior or institutional legislation, but as works of intellect and imagination. This exercise requires attention to rabbinic texts as self-contained works of literature.

The essays below suggest the viability and promise of this procedure. The papers of Neusner and Lightstone graphically illustrate how much can be learned from close attention to the syntactic and formal traits of halakic texts, and the essays on Friedman, Halivni, and Weiss show the virtues and limitations of such literary characteristics in the analysis of talmudic discourse. The texts themselves are presented fully, and although some may find them somewhat demanding, they require no special knowledge to be understood.

An issue of *Semeia* devoted to rabbinic literature is likely to strike at least some regular readers of this journal as uncharacteristic. Yet, the issues described above have affected biblical studies precisely as they have rabbinic scholarship. As new methods steadily deprive biblical and rabbinic texts of their hitherto privileged status, students of both literatures increasingly confront the same epistemological and interpretive problems. Moreover, rabbinic literature represents one of the oldest and most continuous traditions of scriptural interpretation. But before that tradition can effectively assist in the critical examination of the Bible and its literary afterlife, its writing must be read, understood, and analyzed as a literature with its own discourse and its own integrity.

FORM ANALYSIS AND EXEGESIS
The Case of Mishnah Tohorot 2:2-8

Jacob Neusner
Brown University

ABSTRACT

This essay demonstrates the technique of form-analysis as a tool for the exegesis of rabbinic texts. Through a close reading of Mishnah Tohorot 2:2-8, it shows how patterns of language can serve to distinguish primary from secondary elements in a mishnaic pericope and thus how the formulaic patterning of the Mishnah's language constitutes the first sustained commentary to the document itself. Form-analysis therefore can reveal the meaning of mishnaic pericopae to the document's framers.

Form-analysis is the identification of recurrent syntactic patterns in the formulaic language of the Mishnah and the use of those patterns for literary-critical and exegetical purposes. The earliest exegetes of the Mishnah recognized that the language of the document follows disciplined patterns. They knew full well that these patterns at times may serve to indicate the meaning to be assigned to given lemmas. What has been grasped only in current studies is that the formal and formulaic patterning of language in the Mishnah constitutes the first and most important sustained commentary to the Mishnah itself. Form-analysis is the guide to the original meaning of the framers of the document as we now know it.

One principal contribution of form-analysis is to indicate what issues do, and what issues do not, inhere in the fundamental structure of a pericope. Because of the long history of the use of the Mishnah as a source for law far beyond its clear and explicit language, excluding what does not belong is probably the more important of the two exercises. But when we recognize the care with which the framers of the Mishnah have constructed their lists, laid out their triplets culminating in disputes, set forth contrasts between one proposition and its linguistically and conceptually matched opposite, and otherwise expressed their ideas with exquisite care, we grasp the proposition at hand.

In this paper I have chosen one of the most difficult units in the entire Mishnah, Mishnah Tohorot 2:2–8. In this example of how I believe the document must be interpreted, I indicate how the Mishnah's linguistic and syntactic patterns supply the key to its primary meaning. For the present purpose, the Tosefta is mostly ignored, since at only one point is it essential for the interpretation of the corresponding pericope of the Mishnah. I begin with an overview of the entire text and then turn to an analysis of its components.

The Text

Mishnah Tohorot 2:2–8

M. 2:2 A. R. Eliezer [C: Leazar] says, "(1) He who eats food unclean in the first remove is unclean in the first remove;

"(2) [he who eats] food unclean in the second remove is unclean in the second remove;

"(3) [he who eats] food unclean in the third remove is unclean in the third remove."

B. R. Joshua says, "(1) He who eats food unclean in the first remove and food unclean in the second remove is unclean in the second remove.

"(2) [He who eats food] unclean in the third remove is unclean in the second remove so far as Holy Things are concerned,

"(3) and is not unclean in the second remove so far as heave-offering is concerned.

C. "[We speak of] the case of [N, Pa, P, K, Katsh #117, C, Maimonides' text lack:] unconsecrated food

D. "which is prepared in conditions appropriate to heave-offering."

M. 2:3 A. *Unconsecrated food*:
in the first remove is unclean and renders unclean;

B. in the second remove is unfit, but does not convey uncleanness;

C. and in the third remove is eaten in the pottage of heave-offering.

M. 2:4 A. *Heave-offering*:
in the first and in the second remove is unclean and renders unclean;

B. in the third remove is unfit and does not convey uncleanness;

C. and in the fourth remove is eaten in a pottage of Holy Things.

M. 2:5   A. *Holy Things*:
         in the first and the second and the third removes are susceptible to uncleanness and render unclean;
     B. and in the fourth remove are unfit and do not convey uncleanness;
     C. and in the fifth remove are eaten in a pottage of Holy Things.

M. 2:6   A. *Unconsecrated food*:
         in the second remove renders unconsecrated liquid unclean and renders foods of heave-offering unfit.
     B. *Heave-offering*:
        in the third remove renders unclean [the] liquid of Holy Things, and renders foods of Holy Things unfit,
     C. if it [the heave-offering] was prepared in the condition of cleanness pertaining to Holy Things.
     D. But if it was prepared in conditions pertaining to heave-offering, it renders unclean at two removes and renders unfit at one remove in reference to Holy Things.

M. 2:7   A. R. Eleazar [*Eliezer*: GRA, Rosh, V,N,M; *Eleazar* (Leazar): MA, K, Katsh #117, C, Pa, P, PB] says, "The three of them are equal:
     B. "*Holy Things and heave-offering, and unconsecrated food:*
        "which are at the first remove of uncleanness render unclean at two removes and unfit at one [further] remove in respect to Holy Things;
        "render unclean at one remove and spoil at one [further] remove in respect to heave-offering;
        "and spoil unconsecrated food.
     C. "That which is unclean in the second remove in all of them renders unclean at one remove and unfit at one [further] remove in respect to Holy Things;
        "and renders liquid of unconsecrated food unclean;
        "and spoils foods of heave-offering.
     D. "The third remove of uncleanness in all of them renders liquids of Holy Things unclean,
        "and spoils food of Holy Things."

M. 2:8   A. He who eats food unclean in the second remove should not work (*y'šh*; alternate reading: *y'śm*) in the olive press [since he will render the oil unclean].
     B. And unconsecrated food which is prepared in accord with the rules pertaining to Holy Things—lo, this is like unconsecrated food.

C. R. Eleazar b. R. Ṣadoq says, "Lo, it is like heave-offering,
D. "conveying uncleanness at two removes and rendering unfit at one [further] remove."

Overview

M. Tohorot 2:2-8 presupposes knowledge of the rabbinic system of ritual purity. A review of some of its essential elements is necessary for an understanding of the arguments and analyses that follow.

In the rabbinic system, ritual impurity is acquired by contact with either a primary or a secondary source of uncleanness, called a "Father" or a "Child" or "Offspring" of uncleanness, respectively. In the first category are contact with a corpse, a person suffering a flux, a leper, and the like. Objects made of metal, wood, leather, bone, cloth, or sacking become Fathers of uncleanness if they touch a corpse.

Foodstuffs and liquids are susceptible to uncleanness, but will not render other foodstuffs unclean in the same degree or remove of uncleanness that they themselves suffer. Foodstuffs furthermore will not make vessels or utensils unclean. But liquids made unclean by a Father of uncleanness will do so if they touch the inner side of the vessel. That is, if they fall into the contained space of an earthenware vessel, they make the whole vessel unclean.

Food or liquid that touches a Father of uncleanness becomes unclean in the *first* remove. If food touches a person or vessel made unclean by a primary cause of uncleanness, it is unclean in the *second* remove. Food that touches *second* grade uncleanness incurs *third* grade uncleanness, and food that touches *third* grade uncleanness incurs *fourth* grade uncleanness, and so on. But liquids touching either a primary source of uncleanness (Father) or something unclean in the first or second remove (Offspring) are regaded as unclean in the first remove. They are able to make something else unclean. If, for example, the outer side of a vessel is made unclean by a liquid—thus unclean in the second remove—and another liquid touches the outer side, the other liquid incurs not second, but first degree uncleanness.

Heave-offering (food raised up for priestly use only) unclean in the third remove of uncleanness, and Holy Things (that is, things belonging to the cult) unclean in the fourth remove, do not make other things, whether liquids or foods, unclean.

The difference among removes of uncleanness is important. First degree uncleanness in common food will convey uncleanness. But, although food unclean in the second remove will be unacceptable, it will not convey uncleanness, that is, third degree uncleanness. But it will render heave-offering *unfit*.

Further considerations apply to heave-offering and Holy Things.

Heave-offering can be made unfit and unclean by a first, and unfit by a second, degree of uncleanness. If it touches something unclean in the third remove, it is made unfit, but itself will not impart fourth degree uncleanness. A Holy Thing that suffers uncleanness in the first, second, or third remove is unclean and conveys uncleanness. If it is unclean in the fourth remove, it is invalid for the cult but does not convey uncleanness. It is much more susceptible than are noncultic things. Thus, common food that suffers second degree uncleanness will render heave-offering invalid. We already know that it makes liquid unclean in the first remove. Likewise, heave-offering unclean in the third remove will make Holy Things invalid and put them into a fourth remove of uncleanness.

Complications in the system will arise if common food is prepared in conditions of cleanness appropriate for either heave-offering or Holy Things. In that case it will be necessary to determine the status of the food and its susceptibility to uncleanness. This matter is raised in the pericopae discussed below.

With these data firmly in hand, let us turn to a general discussion of M. Toh. 2:2-8.

M. 2:2 introduces the removes of uncleanness. Our interest is in the contaminating affect, upon a person, of eating unclean food. Does the food make the person unclean in the same remove of uncleanness as is borne by the food itself? Thus if one eats food unclean in the first remove, is he unclean in that same remove? This is the view of Eliezar. Joshua says he is unclean in the second remove. The dispute, M. 2:2A-B, at M. 2:2C-D is significantly glossed. The further consideration is introduced as to the sort of food under discussion. Joshua is made to say that there is a difference between the contaminating affects upon the one who eats heave-offering, on the one side, and unconsecrated food prepared in conditions of heave-offering, on the other. This matter, the status of unconsecrated food prepared as if it were heave-offering, or as if it were Holy Things, and heave-offering prepared as if it were Holy Things, forms a substratum of our chapter, added to several primary items and complicating their exegesis. T. 2:1 confirms, however, that primary to the dispute between Eliezer and Joshua is simply the matter of the affects of food unclean in the first remove upon the person who eats such food. The gloss, M. 2:2C-D, forms a redactional-thematic link between Joshua's opinion and the large construction of M. 2:3-7.

M. 2.3:5, expanded and glossed by M. 2:6, follow a single and rather tight form. The sequence differentiates unconsecrated food, heave-offering, and Holy Things each at the several removes from the original source of uncleanness.

Eleazar, M. 2:7, insists that, at a given remove, all three are subject to the *same* rule. The contrary view, M. 2:3-6, is that unconsecrated food in the first remove makes heave-offering unclean and at the second remove spoils heave-offering; it does not enter a third remove and therefore has no affect upon Holy Things. Heave-offering at the first two removes may produce contaminating effects, and at the third remove spoils Holy Things, but is of no effect at the fourth. Holy Things in the first three removes produce uncleanness, and at the fourth impart unfitness to other Holy Things. M. 2:6 then goes over the ground of unconsecrated food at the second remove, and heave-offering at the third. The explanation of M. 2:6C is various; the simplest view is that the clause glosses M. 2:6B by insisting that the heave-offering to which we refer is prepared as if it were Holy Things, on which account, at the third remove, it can spoil Holy Things.

At M. 2:7, as I said, Eleazar restates matters, treating all three—Holy Things, heave-offering, and unconsecrated food—as equivalent to one another at the first, second, and third removes, with the necessary qualification for unconsecrated food that it is like the other, consecrated foods in producing effects at the second and even the third removes. Some commentators read *Eliezer*. They set the pericope up against Joshua's view at M. 2:2, assigning to Joshua M. 2:3ff. as well. My picture of the matter is significantly different from the established exegesis.

M. 2:8 is a singleton. First, we go over the matter on which Joshua and Eliezer agree at M. 2:2, which is that one who eats food unclean in the second remove is unclean in that same remove. Accordingly, he can make liquid unclean, and it is unclean in the first remove. Therefore he should not work in the olive press, since he will make the oil unclean. Then we raise the issue which, as we have seen, recurs in the earlier pericopae but never is wholly spelled out in one place as an integrated problem: What is the rule if we prepare unconsecrated food as if it were Holy Things? M. 2:8B says it remains in the status of unconsecrated food. Eleazar b. R. Ṣadoq says it is like heave-offering. Our chapter does not contain the view that it indeed is like Holy Things. Yet one way of harmonizing M. 2:7 with M. 2:3-6 would be to assert that Eleazar holds the unconsecrated food of which he speaks has, in fact, been prepared as if it were Holy Things, which accounts for the fact that it produces the same effects as do Holy Things.

Thus, one persistent exercise in our chapter is the introduction of the differentiation between unconsecrated food, on the one hand, and unconsecrated food prepared in accord with the rules of cleanness applicable to heave-offering, and, further, to Holy Things, on the other. The issue is intruded, in particular, at M. 2:2, 6, and 8. At M. 2:2, it is surely secondary to the dispute between Eliezer and Joshua, as shown both by form-critical considerations and by T.'s version of the problem under discussion. As to the former, Eliezer says that which is unclean in the first remove makes a person who eats it unclean in the first remove, and so with the second and third. Joshua's theory matches Eliezer's in formal articulation. If one eats something unclean in the first remove, he himself becomes unclean in the second. To be sure, he agrees that if one eats something unclean in the second remove, he too is unclean in the second remove. But, T. explains, that is because what is unclean in the second remove makes the spit in his mouth—liquid—unclean in the first remove, and that in turn makes *him* unclean in the second. Then comes the intrusion, "in respect to unconsecrated food prepared in accord with the rules of cleanness applicable to heave-offering." MSS variants give, further, "*heave-offering* prepared in accord, etc.," that is, omitting *unconsecrated food*. On the face of it, this formal issue is secondary, as I said, and T. knows nothing of it. But reading it as part of Joshua's saying, we have then to interpret the whole pericope to deal with two problems.

The second of these problems is the preparation of food in accord with rules of cleanness not applicable to it, *unconsecrated food* as heave-offering, M. 2:6; *heave-offering* prepared as Holy Things; and, M. 2:8, *unconsecrated food* prepared as Holy Things—the three possibilities. The three are not assembled in a single pericope, rather, added as a layer to the several primary rulings and disputes.

Naturally, the further exegetical problem will be raised, in the Talmuds, about whether we regard the unconsecrated food prepared as it were heave-offering, or the heave-offering prepared as if it were Holy Things, as *wholly* subject to the rules applicable to the higher degree of sanctity, or as only *partially* subject to those rules.

It remains to ask, Is it possible that the issue of unconsecrated food prepared in conditions of cleanness required for heave-offering, and heave-offering prepared in conditions of cleanness required for Holy Things, has been intruded because of some sort of difficulty in the process of transmission of the primary pericopae to which it is attached?

A comparison of M. 2:2 and M. 2:6 makes this seem unlikely. The relationship between the segments is unmistakeable, and each item means what it says. M. 2:2C–D speaks of *unconsecrated food* prepared under the conditions of cleanness required for *heave-offering*, and M. 2:6 clearly wishes to speak of *heave-offering* prepared under the rules of cleanness required for *Holy Things*. There is no repetition of the same words in the two pericopae, which might lead to the conclusion that they do not belong in one or the other unit. The issue is clearly secondary in both pericopae, but is formulated with precision.

To which stratum shall we assign the several pericopae of the chapter?

Let us begin with M. 2:2. Here Joshua and Eliezer debate a fundamental point, the affect of eating unclean food upon the person who eats the food. Is he in the same remove of uncleanness as is the food he eats? Shall we assign to that same stratum the issue of the rules for unconsecrated food prepared *as if* it were heave-offering? It is difficult to know. Since Eleazar b. R. Ṣadoq treats the parallel matter—unconsecrated food

D. "The third remove of uncleanness in all of them renders
liquids of Holy Things unclean,
"and spoils foods of Holy Things."

What is now to be done, before reviewing the interpretation of the pericope in the light of the great commentaries, is to ask, If we had no prepared agendum of questions and no preconceptions, formed on the basis of other rules, what should we understand by the present set of rules? The first, M. 2:3, tells us that unconsecrated food in the first remove from the original source of uncleanness is unclean and renders unclean. That language seems to me to mean exactly what is says, which is that unconsecrated food in the first remove is capable of a further affect of contamination, so that what touches unclean unconsecrated food in the first remove, thus in the second remove, is unclean—unclean, and unfit. Unconsecrated food in the second remove is unfit but does not convey uncleanness. Does heave-offering appear? Obviously not. The simple meaning, therefore, is that unconsecrated food in the second remove is unfit for consumption, presumably by people who wish to keep the laws of cleanness. Unconsecreated food in the third remove produces no contamination. The entire interest of the pericope, therefore, is in unconsecrated food. M. 2:4 then speaks of heave-offering and tells us that heave-offering in the first and second removes are unclean and impart uncleanness. To what do they impart uncleanness? To heave-offering, in the third remove. And that heave-offering is unfit, as we know. The same is to be said of Holy Things. They impart uncleanness at three removes. Accordingly, unconsecrated food produces not two further removes of contamination, but three.

The first remove at M. 2:3 makes something it touches unclean. What it touches should be that which is unclean—in the second remove. But we are told, explicitly, that what is unclean in the second remove is *unfit*, but does not convey uncleanness. The difficult point, therefore, is the second remove. What we should want, for M. 2:3B, if dictated by M. 2:3A, should make provision for the uncleanness referred to at M. 2:3A, and we should have:

Unconsecrated food which is unclean in the first remove is unclean
and conveys uncleanness
Unconsecrated food which is in the second remove is unclean
but does not convey uncleanness
That which is unclean in the third remove . . .

What is somewhat confusing is replacing the *ṭm'* of M. 2:3A with *pśwl* at M. 2:3B (and the same with the parallels of M. 2:4–5). Why has the model of M. 2:3A been abandoned at B? For the contrast clearly is between *unclean/renders unclean* and *unclean/does not render unclean*. Why substitute *unfit* for *unclean* at B and not at A? The question applies to M. 2:7, *render unclean* at two removes and *unfit* at one [third] remove. This bears the same redundancy. If we said only, *render unclean at two removes*, it would follow that what is at the third remove does not *render unclean*—but it *is* unclean. In other words, at the foundation of the shift in language is the evident purpose of marking the end of a chain of contaminating contacts with *unfit*, rather than *unclean*, thus *mṭm'* . . . *pswl* . . . , rather than M. 2:3A's *ṭm'* . . . *mṭm'*. Notice, moreover, that Maimonides uses both word choices (*Other Fathers of Uncleanness* 11:2B) "And whence do we learn that food stuff suffering *second grade uncleanness* is *invalid* . . . ?" I cannot imagine why, except for mnemonic reasons, someone should have shifted the usage, but it is done consistently.

Let us now ask a much more important question: Do M. 2:3–6 continue the opinion of Joshua at M. 2:2? He says that one who eats food unclean in the first and second remove is unclean in the second remove. Will he agree with M. 2:3, assuming we speak of unconsecrated food? Of course he will, because M. 2:3 is of the view that unconsecrated food at the second remove is unfit/unclean. But what do we gain—for Eliezer, M. 2:2A2, says exactly the same thing. Only if we insist that Eleazar at M. 2:7 is Eliezer of M. 2:2 shall we assume that there is disagreement between Eliezer and Joshua on the issues of the present pericope. This brings us to the main point I here contribute. The disagreement is between M. 2:3–6 and M. 2:7, as follows:

M. 2:3	M. 2:7
Unconsecrated food unclean in the first remove:	Unconsecrated food unclean at the first remove:
Contact 1: Unclean, imparts uncleanness at	Contact 1: Unclean, imparts uncleanness at
Contact 2: Unfit (= unclean, but does not impart uncleanness; there is no contact 3)	Contact 2: Unclean, imparts uncleanness at
	Contact 3: Unfit *in respect to Holy Things*
	Contact 1: Unclean, imparts uncleanness at
	Contact 2: Unfit (= unclean, etc.) *in respect to heave-offering*
	Contact 1: Spoils *unconsecrated food* (=makes it unclean, but it does not impart uncleanness; there is no contact 2)

If we assume that M. 2:3–6 are talking, at M. 2:3, about the affects of unconsecrated food *upon* unconsecrated food, then the difference between M. 2:3 and M. 2:7 (Eleazar) is very clear. Eleazar is of the view that unconsecrated food in the first remove does not impart uncleanness at all. It may *become* unclean, but it has no affect upon other food.

What sort of food does have an impact upon other food? Only heave-offering and Holy Things. They indeed do produce the affect of uncleanness/unfitness, and may further produce the affect of such severe contamination that a further stage of contamination is possible.

If that indeed is Eleazar's view, then to whom will it be important to insist that, when unconsecrated food does have the capacity to impart uncleanness, it is in fact unconsecrated food which has been prepared under conditions of cleanness required for heave-offering—to whom, if not to Eleazar! The gloss of M. 2:2C–D in fact brings Joshua into conformity with Eleazar's quite separate point, by making him say that, when he speaks of food in the first, second, and third removes producing uncleanness, it is specifically unconsecrated food prepared under conditions of cleanness required for heave-offering. But why should Joshua alone be made to say so? For Eliezer of M. 2:2 has told us that he who eats food unclean in the first remove is unclean in the first remove—which is to say, unclean food imparts uncleanness. So C–D must in fact be read as (Eleazar's) glosses of both Eliezer's and Joshua's total and completed dispute.

What about the equivalent gloss at M. 2:6? There we are told that heave-offering prepared in conditions of cleanness required for Holy Things when in the third remove produces uncleanness—that is, it makes fluids of Holy Things unclean and renders food of Holy Things unfit. (To put it otherwise, the liquid falls into the first remove and so has the capacity to render other things unclean, but the solid food does not, so is merely unclean itself, without further contaminating capacity.) What is Eleazar's view of the capacity of heave-offering to render something unclean? At M. 2:7D, he speaks of the third remove of "the three of them" (including heave-offering). What does it do? It renders unclean liquids of Holy Things and renders unfit food of Holy Things (!). Does Eleazar disagree with M. 2:6? Of course not—that is, *if* we include the gloss of M. 2:6C: heave-offering at the third remove renders liquid of Holy Things unclean and foods of Holy Things unfit.

What is it that the glosses accomplish?

First, they eliminate the dispute (?) between Eleazar and Joshua and Eliezer of M. 2:2, on the one side.

Second, they force M. 2:6 to concur with Eleazar.

And what is Eleazar's position in these matters? In his view, the unconsecrated food not prepared as if it were heave-offering and the heave-offering not prepared as if it were Holy Things has precisely the same contaminating power as if it were prepared in accord with the more strict set of rules, respectively.

At issue, then, is nothing other than the (unstated) agendum of our chapter, the capacity to raise food to a higher order of sensitivity to uncleanness by subjecting it to rules of cleanness not ordinarily required, unconsecrated food to heave-offering, heave-offering to Holy Things. That which is not essential at M. 2:2, 6, (and 8) in fact has shaped the articulation of the whole set, M. 2:2–8. If the fact is that M. 2:2C–D serve as a gloss, to bring that set into relationship to Eleazar's opinion, then what shall we isolate as the equivalent gloss to the set M. 2:3–6? The answer is obvious: the whole of M. 2:6 serves to gloss M. 2:3–5 in much the same way as M. 2:2C–D revise M. 2:2A–B.

Who is this Eleazar, who holds that it makes no difference whether we prepare unconsecrated food as unconsecrated food, or whether we prepare it as heave-offering, and whether we prepare heave-offering as such, or whether we prepare it as Holy Things? It is none other than the authority of M. 2:8B, who tells us that if we prepare unconsecrated food as if it were Holy Things, it has exactly the same capacity to impart uncleanness as other unconsecrated food. Eleazar b. R. Ṣadoq, who holds that unconsecrated food prepared as if it were Holy Things produces the contaminating affects of heave-offering, will differ. And we have, in fact, an Ushan construction, between Eleazar b. R. Ṣadoq and an Ushan Eleazar (or Eliezer, it hardly matters among Ushans) on exactly the same point.

And why is it that Eleazar takes this position? Because, so far as he is concerned, what is important is not the source of contamination— the unclean foods—but that which is contaminated, the unconsecrated food, heave-offering, and Holy Things.

He could not state matters more clearly than he does when he says that the three of them are exactly equivalent. And they are, because the differentiations will emerge in the food affected, or contaminated, by the three. So at the root of the dispute is whether we gauge the contamination in accord with the source—unconsecrated food, or unconsecrated food prepared as if it were heave-offering, and so on—or whether the criterion is the food which is contaminated. M. 2:3–5 are all wrong, Eleazar states explicitly at M. 2:7A, because they differentiate among uncleanness imparted by unclean unconsecrated food, unclean heave-offering, and unclean Holy Things, and do not differentiate among the three sorts of food *to which* contamination is imparted.

It is surely a logical position, for the three sorts of food do exhibit differentiated capacities to receive uncleanness; one sort *is* more contaminable than another. And so too is the contrary view logical: *what is more sensitive to uncleanness also will have a greater capacity to impart uncleanness.* The subtle debate before us clearly is unknown to Eliezer and Joshua at M. 2:2. To them the operative categories are something unclean in first, second, or third *removes,* without distinction as to the relative sensitivities of the several types of food which may be unclean.

The sequence thus begins with Eliezer and Joshua, who ask about the contaminating power of that which is unclean in the first and second removes, without regard to whether it is unconsecrated food, heave-offering, or Holy Things. To the, the distinction between the capacity to impart contamination, or to receive contamination, of the several sorts of food is unknown. Once, however, their question is raised—in such general terms—it will become natural to ask the next logical question, one which makes distinctions not only among the several removes of uncleanness, but also among the several sorts of food involved in the processes of contamination. That step is not before us. Only the still further, logical extension of the issue *is* before us, the third dimension in our three-dimensional construction: (1) removes, three; (2) types of food, three; and, finally, (3) whether the important aspect of the types of food is its susceptibility to *receive* uncleanness or its capacity to *impart* uncleanness, three respectively. Each system—Eleazar's and the authority of M. 2:3-5's—bears twenty-seven possibilities, therefore, with the difference in the systems coming in at the 18th through 27th cases, so to speak. Our picture of the matter will intersect with the inherited one, but also come into conflict, for fairly obvious reasons.

M. 2:8

A. He who eats food unclean in the second remove should not work (*yʿśh*; alt.: *yʿśm*) in the olive press, [since he will render the oil unclean].

B. And unconsecrated food which is prepared in accord with the rules pertaining to Holy Things—lo, this is like unconsecrated food.

C. R. Eleazar b. R. Ṣadoq says, "Lo, it is like heave-offering,

D. "conveying uncleanness at two removes and rendering unfit at one [further] remove."

A is separate from B–C. Why should a person who has eaten food unclean in the second remove not work in the olive press? Because the olive oil will emerge. The person is unclean in the second remove, as both Eliezer and Joshua will agree, and he will render the liquid unclean in the first remove. This will render the press unclean (T. 1:7C).

B now returns to the issue of M. 2:2C–D. There we are told that unconsecrated food which is prepared in accord with the rules of the cleanness of heave-offering produces a third remove, just as does heave-offering. B now adds that unconsecrated food prepared in accord with the rules pertaining to the cleanness of Holy Things is unchanged and remains adjudged in accord with the rules, for the cleanness and removes from uncleanness, of unconsecrated food, and with those alone. That matter is not raised at M. 2:2C–D, nor does it occur at M. 2:6. The former tells us about unconsecrated food prepared as if it were heave-offering.

The latter speaks of heave-offering prepared as if it were Holy Things. So we can raise each level by one: (1) unconsecrated food to heave-offering; (2) heave-offering to Holy Things. But (3) we cannot raise the first to the third level.

Eleazar b. R. Ṣadoq says that if we treat unconsecrated food as if it were Holy Things, to be sure it does not fall into the category of Holy Things. But it *does* fall into the category of heave-offering and becomes subject to its rules of contamination, the other possible position. What is curious is that these matters are not put together into a single pericope but scattered among the several as glosses.

FORM AS MEANING IN HALAKIC *MIDRASH*
A Programmatic Statement

Jack N. Lightstone
Concordia University

ABSTRACT

This essay proposes a new method for the study of rabbinic *midrash*. Conventional methods define *midrash* functionally and study it diachronically. By failing to treat midrashic compilations as whole documents, they ignore the specifically literary aspects of *midrash*, such as form and structure. An analysis of the form of *Masekta dePisha, Bo* 8 of the *Mekilta deRabbi Ishmael*, a form typical of the entire document, reveals a rabbinic theory of the nature of Scripture that could not be deduced from the document's content. That theory holds that *halakah* (rabbinic praxis) is immanent in Scripture but can be derived only if Scripture is regarded and read as an organic whole, in which all parts interact.

The halakic *midrashim* have been the object of sustained scholarly interest since the earliest days of the *Wissenschaft des Judenthums*. Before the mid-1940s, two sorts of study dominated research on these and other midrashic writings: the philological and anthological. The former produced scholarly editions of texts and attempted to date documents. The latter generated collections primarily of aggadic *midrashim* organized either by theme or to parallel the order of verses in Scripture.[1] But the interest of the *Wissenschaft* in *midrash*, particularly in halakic *midrash*, had historical implications. Scholars came to believe that the halakic *midrashim*, more than the Mishnah, the Tosefta, or the Talmuds, preserved rabbinism's most ancient literary expressions.[2] Most students of *midrash*

---

[1] For a review of the modern study of midrash, see G. G. Porton, "Midrash: Palestinian Jews and the Hebrew Bible in the Greco-Roman Period," in H. Temporini, W. Hasse, eds., *Aufstieg und Niedergang der römischen Welt*, II. 19.2 (Berlin: de Gruyter, 1979).

[2] See J. Z. Lauterbach, "Midrash and Mishnah," *JQR*, 1915, reprinted in J. Z. Lauterbach, *Rabbinic Essays* (Cincinnati: Hebrew Union College Press, 1951); see also H. Albeck, *Mavo LeMishnah* (Tel Aviv: Dvir, 1959), pp. 41ff.

agreed that the present form of the Mishnah antedates the extant versions and editions of halakic *midrashim*. But the theory that *midrash* as a literary genre represented an earlier stage of rabbinic literature than the "mishanic format" nevertheless found substantial support.[3] In the rabbinic method of squeezing *halakah* out of Scripture, the *Wissenschaft* preceived the solution to its principal problem: Whence and by what means did rabbinic Judaism come into being?[4]

Whatever its appeal, there is little evidence for the hypothesis of midrashic primacy. The halakic *midrash* in rabbinic documents cannot be shown to be earlier than the second century C.E. Indeed, most of it seems to derive from the third century.[5] The claim that the midrashic form is significantly earlier, despite the absence of datable exemplars, ignores the evidence in favor of self-serving speculation.[6]

Despite the weakness of these historical claims, the *Wissenschaft's* distinction between midrashic and mishnaic "format" rests on solid literary data. But these data have hardly affected the scholarly study of *midrash*. Although the philologists of the *Wissenschaft* identified the formulaic traits of rabbinic documents, they and their successors were unable, for various reasons, to appropriate the questions and techniques of biblical form-criticism and form-history.[7] Instead they followed the path of tradition-history.

The current direction in midrashic studies was established shortly after World War II by a circle of scholars variously reacting to the work

---

[3] Lauterbach, "Midrash and Mishnah"; Albeck, *Mavo'*.

[4] Again these concerns are aptly documented by Lauterbach, "Midrash and Mishnah," and by Albeck, *Mavo'*. For a general account of the *Wissenschaft des Judentums*, see I. Schorsch, "Ideology and History," in H. Graetz, *The Structure of Jewish History and other Essays*, I. Schorsch, ed. and trans. (New York: Jewish Theological Seminary/Ktav, 1975).

[5] Needless to say, there are widely variant datings of individual documents. For some idea of the range of proposals, see M. D. Herr, "Midrashei Halakah," *Encyclopaedia Judaica*, XI *(Jerusalem: Keter, 1971)*. With regard to the *Mekilta deRabbi Ishmael* in particular, see B. Z. Wacholder's article in the *HUCA* of 1968. In proposing an 8th Century date for the document, Wacholder represents one extreme view. A convenient summary of opinions on the date of the *Mekilta* may be found in E. P. Sanders, *Paul and Palestinian Judaism* (London: SCM, 1977), pp. 65ff.

[6] None of this is intended to deny that rabbinic Judaism has its origins in biblical religion. But to claim that *midrash* constitutes the model by which the one generated the other begs a whole range of questions about how early rabbinism or proto-rabbinism perceived its relationship to Scripture, and about the nature of rabbinic authority relative to that Scripture.

[7] See K. Koch, *The Growth of the Biblical Tradition: The Form-Critical Method* (New York: Scribner's, 1969); R. Bultmann, *The History of the Synoptic Tradition*[2] (New York: Harper & Row, 1968); G. M. Tucker, *Form Criticism of the Old Testament* (Philadelphia: Fortress, 1971).

of Renée Bloch.⁸ Bloch was interested in the history and cultural meaning of *midrash*. She turned away from philological and literary questions and defined *midrash* in terms of its contemporizing function. For her, the historical study of *midrash* should trace midrashic traditions through time in order to specify and elucidate the array of meanings given to a particular segment of Scripture. Bloch's "description" of *midrash*, now virtually authoritative, is reported by Wright as follows:

> Renée Bloch . . . has defined rabbinic midrash as a homiletical reflection or meditation of the Bible which seeks to reinterpret or actualize a given text of the past for present circumstances. Then in her discussion of biblical material . . . she classifies each of the following as midrash: historical works which gloss Scripture for instruction and edification; a meditation on history, tending to give to this history a relevance for contemporary preoccupations; a re-use of traditional sacred texts with a religious reflection on their content and on the past to which they witness, making them relevant for the contemporary situation . . . ; the use of scriptural texts for the purpose of edification in the light of contemporary needs; a work which alludes to earlier history and suppresses, embellishes and rearranges the traditional account and imposes a new meaning on them; a work with a scriptural reminiscence which proceeds entirely from a meditation on Scripture; a development on OT texts. . . .⁹

Bloch's characterization of *midrash* implies certain formal–literary traits. To be *midrash*, a text would have to refer back to, even if it did not cite, some antecedent oral or written tradition. Beyond this minimal literary criterion, all requisites of *midrash* seem functional. Any midrashic piece must "contemporize" its antecedent tradition for the believing community. In such an operation, the meaning of the tradition is simultaneously preserved and subtly transformed to speak to the contemporary situation.

Bloch's functional definition of *midrash* effected some startlingly fresh approaches in scholarship. Her outlook encouraged interest in the history of traditions and in their reinterpretation over extended periods of time within the living community. It also provoked a sensitivity to the relationship between midrashic interpretations and the problems the community faced. Bloch's studies raised, albeit sometimes indirectly, the question of continuity and change within the religious traditions under analysis.

---

⁸ R. Bloch, "Midrash," *Dictionnaire de la Bible*, Suppl., Fasc. XXIX (Paris, 1957); R. Bloch, "Note méthodologique pour l'étude de la litterature rabbinique," *Recherches des Sciences Religieuses*, XLIII (Paris, 1955); G. Vermes, *Post-Biblical Jewish Studies* (Leiden: Brill, 1975); G. Vermes, *Scripture and Tradition* (Leiden: Brill, 1961); A. Wright, *The Literary Genre Midrash* (New York: 1967); see also J. Sanders, *Torah and Canon* (Philadelphia: Fortress, 1972).

⁹ A. Wright, ibid., pp. 19-20.

There is little reason to quarrel with these developments, but one must recognize that such a definition of *midrash* significantly expands its semantic range beyond that of conventional scholarly usage. The methodological side-effects of this terminological shift deserve consideration.

Bloch and others after her found *midrash* in the Bible itself and regarded these biblical *midrashim* as the forerunners of classical rabbinic exegetical literature. The Book of Chronicles was the typical referent. In the work of the Chronicler, the narrative of Genesis through II Kings is reinterpreted in light of the editor's new theology, his particular version of *Heilsgeschichte*. Chronicles satisfies the minimal literary criterion for *midrash* as Bloch defined it, and the document functions as *midrash*. Some would argue that the same may be said not only of entire compilations but also of individual passages that parallel, depend upon, and subtly change other pericopae. Thus, each version of the covenant story would constitute a *midrash* of some antecedent one. Even the oldest identifiable recension would be a *midrash* of the events as they "really happened." On this model, the study of *midrash* is reduced to tradition-history. Whether Bloch fully saw or intended such a consequence, I cannot say. Subsequent scholars did. G. Vermes provides a case in point. He states:

> No one familiar with the Old Testament can fail to observe the repeated emphasis laid by some of its authors on the obligation to meditate on, recite and rethink the Law. It was no doubt a midrashic process such as this which was partly responsible for the formulation of the more recent legal codes, the Deuteronomic and Priestly, and its influence becomes more apparent in post-exilic literature (Chronicles and Daniel) and certain of the Apocrypha (Ecclesiasticus). Post-biblical midrash is to be distinguished from the biblical only by an external factor, canonization.[10]

For Vermes, the midrashic process appears at work within Scripture, much of which itself will have been generated by the midrashic enterprise. Advocates of canonical criticism have pushed Vermes's position to its logical conclusion. J. Sanders,[11] for one, maintains that canonical analysis constitutes the study of *midrash* in so far as each canonical text reinterprets for the community those sets of "meanings" conveyed by some antecedent scriptural tradition. In his opinion, tradition-history, the analysis of *midrash*, and canonical criticism amount essentially to the same endeavor—so long as canonical texts are the object of study.

The insights of Bloch, Vermes, and Sanders have contributed both to the study of tradition-history prior to the canonization of major sections

---

[10] G. Vermes, *Post-Biblical Jewish Studies*, p. 59.
[11] J. Sanders, *Torah and Canon*, see the introduction.

of the Hebrew Scriptures and to our general understanding of the subsequent function of those texts. But, although it elucidates continuities of function and process within the Israelite community, their approach runs roughshod over the variety of means by which contemporization occurs. This is the result of the extension of the term *midrash* to materials other than a specific genre of rabbinic literature.

The functional definition of *midrash* has produced studies that examine vertical slices of successive strata of Israelite and rabbinic literature. Much less has been accomplished on the horizontal or synchronic plane. We lack systematic studies of discrete rabbinic documents that focus on their idiomatic traits of thought and outlook. The functional approach to *midrash* has obstructed such studies because, from its perspective, all midrashic documents are similar at the level of function. The cultural meanings of literary form and of rhetoric receive little attention. For instance, the Mishnah and the halakic *midrashim* represent vastly different types of literary endeavor. But since they both contemporize Scripture, from a functional perspective they constitute exemplars of *midrash*. The significance of the different and distinct literary characteristics of the documents is ignored.

The shortfalls of the methods surveyed above suggest the value of a new approach. In particular, the diachronic approach advocated by Bloch and her successors must be complemented with a synchronic one. Midrashic documents must be dissected and interpreted as literary "wholes" in their own right. Their provenance, their traits of thought and world-view, and their formal and redactional characteristics deserve scholarly attention. Only in this way can we discern if the various documents of rabbinic literature make differing statements about the "way things are" or "ought to be," despite their shared assent to the authority of Scripture as a basis for any definition of "the world."[12]

To advocate such an approach does not deny that rabbinic documents are compilations of discrete antecedent materials that each have their own histories. However, systematic analyses of the Mishnah indicate that its editors exercised autonomy in shaping what they received.[13] The Mishnah's tractates constitute structured essays in which the text analyzes the *halakah* with respect to abstract principles. The content and development of the Mishnah largely represent the minds of its penultimate editors.[14] The work of these editors also extends to the language

---

[12] For a fuller discussion of the "systemic approach" to the study of rabbinic literature, see J. Lightstone, "Problems and New Perspectives in the Study of Early Rabbinic Ethics," *Journal of Religious Ethics*, Fall (1981).

[13] J. Neusner, *A History of the Mishnaic Law of Purities*, XXI (Leiden: Brill, 1977); see also part XXII of the same.

[14] See J. Neusner, *Judaism: The Evidence of the Mishnah* (Chicago: University of Chicago Press, 1981).

and formulation of mishnaic pericopae.[15] Any analysis of the Mishnah that bypasses this synchronic approach will seriously fail to understand the character, function, and meaning of the compilation.

The systematic analysis of the Mishnah establishes a new direction for the study of the halakic *midrashim* and for a critical inquiry into the thought and world-view of their editors and compilers. Such a study must take seriously the hypothesis that the redactors have communicated their ideas not merely by preserving what they received but also by selecting their materials and by shaping their sources into a new "whole."

A consideration of the more obvious ways redactors left their marks on the materials they used will help to identify the locus of inquiry into the "meanings" conveyed by the documents themselves or by their major sub-units. Even a cursory reading of halakic *midrashim* will show that the redactors of these texts take great pains to formally present scripture as the source from which *halakah* emerges. The persistence of this literary trait even when the relationship between the verse and its halakic interpretation is forced, strained, or dissonant, suggests that for the redactors of these documents the form of the text held an importance that often outweighed matters of content and meaning. Such intentional and repetitive literary "behavior" demands interpretation. The way the producers of these documents chose to express themselves is integral to their view of the place and meaning of the biblical tradition in their rabbinic vision of the "Israelite world." In other words, the form and rhetoric of halakic *midrash* appears to be a central component of the "message" of the literature. A method appropriate to the exegesis of the "ways of saying things" will, therefore, direct attention not merely to the content of midrashic compilations, but also to the formal characteristics of the texts.

A representative example will help to demonstrate both the plausibility of these claims and their implications. Let us turn, then, to *Masekta dePisha*, *Bo* 8 of the *Mekilta deRabbi Ishmael*.

The passage of the *Mekilta* takes as its point of departure the injunction at Exod 12:15 against eating leaven on the Passover.

> Seven days you shall eat unleavened bread; on the first day (*'k b'wm hr'šwn*) you shall put away leaven out of your houses. (Exod 12:15)

It is concerned in particular with the words, "on the first day."

    A. "'On the first day, etc.'—
    B. "[this means] beginning with (*'m*) the eve of the holy day.
    C. "Do you say [the verse means] beginning with the eve of the holy day, or might it not be [Scripture's intent that leaven be removed] on the holy day itself?

---

[15] See note 13.

D. "Scripture says, 'You shall not offer the blood of my sacrifice with leaven' (Exod 34:25).
E. "[That is to say,] do not slaughter the passover [offering on the eve of the festival], while leaven still exists," the words of R. Ishmael.
F. R. Jonathan says, "One does not require the [exegesis based on Exod 34:25].
G. "Lo, it is already stated [at Exod 12:16], 'No work shall be done on those days.'
H. "And burning [the method of destroying leaven] is a type of work.
I. "Therefore, when (mh) Scripture says, 'On the first day,' [its intent is,] beginning with the eve of the holy day."
J. R. Yosé the Galilean says, "'On the first day you shall put away leaven from out of your houses,'
K. "[This means] beginning with the eve of the holy day.
L. "Do you say thus [Oxford and Munich mss.: from the eve of the holy day], or might it not be [Scripture's intent that leaven be removed] on the holy day itself?
M. "Scripture says, 'But (ʾk) on the [first] day.'
N. "[The extra partative informs us that Scripture] differentiates [between two days]."[16]

The passage falls neatly into three major sections: an exegesis of Exod 12:15 (sections A–E) bearing Ishmael's name; the saying attributed to Jonathan (F–I); and a final exegesis attributed to Yosé the Galilean (J–N). The whole has probably been formulated as a unit. F–I, Jonathan's statement, depends upon Ishmael's exegesis and would otherwise be unintelligible. The Yosé-saying (J–N) makes perfectly good sense on its own, but since the language of J–N so carefully matches that of the first section, it is difficult to maintain that Yosé's saying was formulated in some other context. Together, then, the three sections constitute a rather tight and elegant exegetical dispute.

The dispute-form, the formulation of materials as a series of contradictory sayings addressing a single topic, is typical of mishnaic and post-mishnaic rabbinic literature. Its use here, then, seems of no particular value in highlighting the idiomatic traits of halakic *midrash*. Considerably more germane is the internal pattern evident at A–E and J–N. A synoptic chart alerts us to the phenomenon.

	A–E	J–N
1.	———————————	R. Yosé . . . says:
2.	"On the first day" (Exod 12:15)	"On the first day" (Exod 12:15)

[16] *Mekilta deRabbi Ishmael*, ed. Horovitz, p. 27, line 13–p. 28, line 6; cf. *Mek. deR. Simeon* on Ex. 12:15; *bPes.* 5a.

3. beginning with the eve of the holy day	beginning with the eve of the holy day
4. Do you say beginning with the eve of the holy day, or might it not be on the holy day itself	Do you say beginning with the eve of the holy day, or might it not be on the holy day itself
5. Scripture says, "You shall not offer . . ." (Exod 34:25)	Scripture says, "But (*'k*) on the [first] day" (Exod 12:15) [the extra partative informs us that Scripture] differentiates [between two days]
6. do not slaughter the passover while leaven still exists,	
7. the words of R. Ishmael	

With the exception of the attributive formulae at the end of A–E and at the beginning of J–N (sections 1 and 7 respectively), the exegeses betray identical structures. Both open with citations of the verse of Scripture at issue (sec. 2). A statement of the accepted legal interpretation follows (sec. 3). Subsequently (at 4), that normative understanding is called into question by an exegesis that takes a more straightforward, or equally plausible, approach to the verse. In this instance the alternative exegesis asks if it may not reasonably be deduced from Exod 12:15 that leaven is removed on the first day of the festival itself. In response to this challenge, A–E and J–N cite further scriptural evidence (sec. 5), stating finally (sec. 6) how, on the strength of this additional citation, the alternative exegesis must be abandoned in favor of the accepted interpretation. The following pattern emerges:

    1. Scripture a;
    2. means x;
    3. does it mean x,
       or might it not mean y?
    4. but Scripture b;
    5. undermines y,
       and/or supports x.

But what about the middle exegesis attributed to Jonathan? It does not remain "odd man out." In part, F–I reverses the pattern of the other two exegeses, ultimately producing the same effect as A–E and J–N.

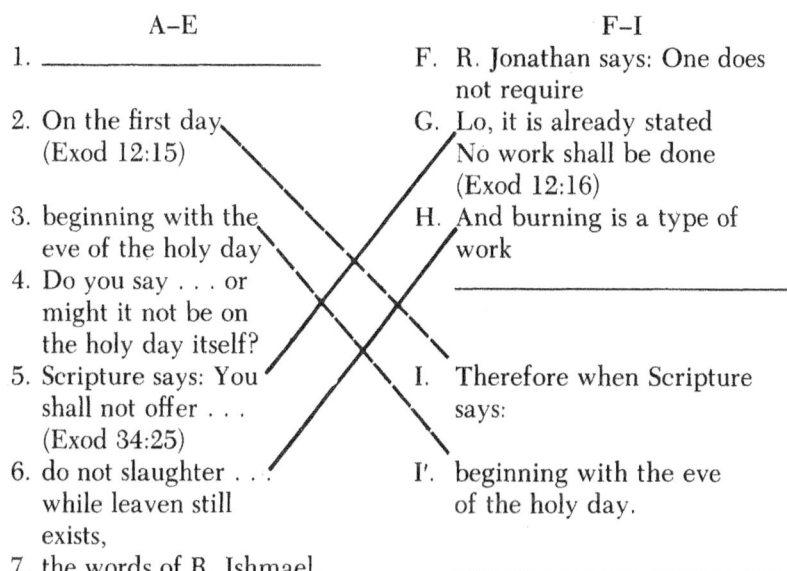

In F–I, one first encounters the additional scriptural data (at G = 2), followed (at H = 3) by an argument against the inappropriate legal view. I (= 5) then concludes with the verse under scrutiny (Exod 12:15) and the standard legal interpretation (I' = 6). Finally, the opening words of the exegesis (F = 1) effect a transition from the previous exegetical saying and introduce Jonathan's exegesis. While F–I's variation of the pattern would indeed prove unintelligible on its own, it aptly, and even elegantly, glosses an antecedent exegesis. In short, the same basic structure appears three times in the pericope (not twice), and the second occasion evinces a not unaesthetic variation of the primary pattern.

It would be remiss to argue for the existence of a structured pattern on the basis of a single pericope. Rules of literary structure, like rules governing language, are implicit. A pattern may be abstracted, only if evident in a number of cases. The structure of *Masekta dePisḥa*, Bo 8 is present in much of the *Mekilta*. The 18 chapters of the tractate provide more than 40 examples of it, including some variations.[17] The structure, moreover,

---

[17] The following is a comprehensive list of passages in *Mesekta dePisḥa* in which the pattern appears (including variations and truncated versions thereof); pages and lines refer to the Horovitz-Rabin edition of the *Mekilta* (Jerusalem: Bamberger and Wahrman, 1960): *Proem*: p. 2, lines 5ff.; *Chapter 1*: p. 6, lines 18ff.; p. 7, lines 11ff.; *Chapter 3*: p. 10, lines 1ff.; p. 10, lines 5ff.; p. 10, lines 10ff.; *Chapter 4*: p. 12, lines 17ff.; p. 13, lines 4ff.; p. 13, lines 9ff.; p. 13, lines 12ff.; p. 13, lines 20ff.; *Chapter 6*: p. 18, lines 9ff.; p. 18, lines 11ff.; p. 19, lines 10ff.; p. 20, lines 8ff.; *Chapter 7*: p. 22, lines 11ff.; p. 22, lines 14ff.; p. 26, lines 8ff.; *Chapter 8*: p. 26, lines 19ff.; p. 27, lines 1ff.; p. 27, lines 13ff.; p. 28, lines 4ff.; p. 28, lines 6ff.; *Chapter 9*: p. 30, lines 19ff.; p. 33, lines 4ff.; *Chapter 10*: p. 34, lines 6ff.; *Chapter 11*: p. 27, line 9; p. 37, lines 10ff.; *Chapter 13*: p. 43, lines 6f.; p. 46, lines

cannot be dismissed as stemming from one particular circle of master and disciples. The passages in question bear the names of a number of rabbis, and it hardly seems possible to associate the pattern with any one man. Indeed, if independent sayings emerging from distinct circles ultimately lie behind such pericopae, little or nothing remains of their language. Any idomatic modes of speech, or formal traits of a particular group of tradents, have been assimilated to one of several variations of relatively few rhetorical patterns. It follows that such formalization took place when independent lines of tradition were combined. In other words, these structures speak for the redactors of the *midrash*, if for anyone. The study of such structures must begin with the work of redactors, with compilations and their constituent sub-units, as opposed to discrete exegeses attributed to individual rabbis.

Structures convey meaning because of law-like rules governing (1) the elements of the structure, (2) the relations among those elements and (3) the range of permissible content of any one element. Such meanings remain distinct from the particular content at any one instance of the structure. In the realm of narrative, the stock plots of films about white men and Indians in the American West provides an apt example.[18] The very fact that we have come to recognize their plots as "stock" implies that we acknowledge a set of meanings (here about relations between, and moral worth of, Whites and Indians) that is distinct from the content of any one movie. Whether it concerns the Apache or the Blackfoot nations, Sitting Bull or Geronimo, the particulars of the plot are immaterial. That law-like rules of the structure convey a world-view is obvious to anyone who has watched children play "Cowboys and Indians." In encountering the pattern on a multitude of occasions, we "experience" these law-like relations as "the way things are in reality," as parts of our world-view.

This argument applies to many midrashic patterns. The elements of

---

8ff.; *Chapter 15*: p. 54, lines 15ff.; p. 55, lines 3ff.; p. 55, lines 8ff.; p. 55, lines 12ff.; *Chapter 16*: p. 61, lines 16ff.; *Chapter 17*: p. 6, lines 4ff. (aggadic); p. 64, lines 10ff.; p. 66, lines 5ff.; p. 66, lines 20ff.; p. 67, lines 1f.; p. 67, lines 3f.; p. 67, lines 5ff.; p. 67, lines 14ff.; p. 68, lines 13ff. As indicated by the noted exception, the pattern is overwhelmingly associated with halakic pericopae. The third element of the pattern in virtually all of these passages commences with the formulary, '*t*' '*mr kn* '*w* '*nw* '*l*'. The reader may be tempted, therefore, to see the structure as integrally tied to such phrases. We must offer in this regard a note of caution. Structures remain implicit in ordered content, where rules may be abstracted which define that order, determine the range and limits of the content and establish relationships between elements of the pattern. None of this necessarily implies the presence of particular formulaic language in every instance. Just as in the dispute-form attributional formulae may vary, so to here, and in all structures, "formulaic equivalents" may readily replace one another. Form (or structure) must not be confused with formularies.

[18] For this example I am indebted to J. D. Crossan, *The Dark Interval* (Niles, Illinois: Argus, 1975).

the structure of *Masekta dePisha, Bo* 8 constitute "pigeon-holes" for the arrangement of content. Their order and the relationships among them appear to be governed by implicit rules. The content of any single "pigeon-hole" may vary, but within certain determined limits. For example, citations in the first element must be from Scripture, indeed, probably from the Torah (Pentateuch) only; but Exod 12:15 need not always be the point of departure. So too, in the second element, one must encounter the "accepted" *halakah*, not some hypothetical legal stance that might equally be conveyed by the verse. Still, one is not limited to *halakah* about removal of leaven on the Passover. The choice of Scripture at the outset determines the content of the second element, just as the choice of the particular Indian tribe in a Western will determine the geographical setting and the name of the chief. But in neither the Western nor our midrashic pattern does the structure *wholly* determine the content. The meaning conveyed by the midrashic pattern stands apart from the particular information offered at any one instance of the structure. The pericope tells one that leaven must be removed on the eve of the Passover and implies that one learns this from Exod 12:15 in conjunction with one of several other verses of Scripture (or the particle, *'k*). But the repetition of the pattern with different verses and other *halakot* makes a statement in itself—a statement about the relationship between *halakah*, Scripture, and the human intellect.

How so? Let us return to our pattern. The structure opens with (a) a citation of the verse of Scripture at issue. This is followed by: (b) the accepted *halakah* that supposedly finds its origins in the verse; (c) the rhetorical questioning of the *halakah* as a correct interpretation of the scriptural injunction (since one might reasonably construe the verse otherwise); (d) citation of other scriptural material (or a more refined look at the verse at hand, as in Yosé's case); and (e) an argument that the new scriptural data rules out the alternative reading or that it explicitly confirms the accepted interpretation.

At one level this midrashic pattern makes a statement that it shares with all other forms of the halakic *midrashim*. The *halakah*—"Oral Torah" at some point in early rabbinic ideology—finds its origins in Scripture (or "Written Torah"). Rabbinic law has no independent status or claim to authority. Such a view flies in the face of what appears to be the Mishnah's position on this question. For the Mishnah, *halakah* rests upon independent divine authority, even when the law merely expands upon Scripture.[19] That such meanings may be attributed to "mishnaic form" and to "midrashic form" is clear from the *Wissenschaft*'s conception of the importance of these formal distinctions. Scholars of the "Science of Judaism" turned the theological statement implicit in "midrashic

---

[19] See. J. Neusner, *Judaism: The Evidence of Mishnah*.

format" into a historical hypothesis. For them, *halakah* was generated out of Scripture and, in the view of many, was first recorded as *midrash halakah*. The *Wissenschaft*'s picture may constitute faulty historical reasoning, but it rests on a sensitivity to the most basic meaning conveyed by midrashic rhetoric.

This paper's methodological prospectus would remain trivial, however, if specific midrashic structures, like that of *Bo* 8, did not make more specific statements of theology or ideology. In our case, that specificity concerns the nature of Scripture, and, more important, its consequences for the exercise of the rabbinic intellect in determining the *halakah*. Taking for granted that rabbinic law is immanent in Torah, the midrashic pattern at hand implies that any one biblical injunction may appear equally amenable to several halakic interpretations. That problem is rendered more acute by the structure when the alternative to the accepted *halakah* appears *prima facie* the more reasonable exegesis of the verse. The first three elements of our pattern, then, define the problematic. The last two effect the resolution by demonstrating that *the halakah*—that single correct "way"—remains immanent, nevertheless, in Scripture as a whole. That is, danger lies not in reason *per se* as a mode of halakic exegesis, but in a misapprehension of Scripture's nature coupled with the exercise of reason. When the exegete fails to understand that all parts of Scripture mutually inform and complement all other parts, his intellectual prowess, even when taking Scripture as his point of departure, will mislead him. If, however, one regards the (Written) Torah as an organic whole in which all parts interact, in which all parts are necessary and none alone suffices to solve a halakic problem, then the halakic enterprise stands on firm ground. Halakic discourse that does not take Scripture, all of Scripture, as its point of departure remains by implication illegitimate or, at least, suspect.[20]

It would be wrong to find in this pattern a critique of the use of reason altogether and a preference for formal exegesis. Neusner has shown this to be the case for *Sifra's* treatment of Mishnah, *Seder Toharot*.[21] But here, the exegeses attributed to Ishmael and Jonathan exhibit a rational and deductive approach to the supplementary verses cited. The structure, however, also attests to the efficacy of other than deductive heremeneutics. The pericope examined above contains an apparently deliberate progression of the scriptural material used to support the accepted *halakah*. A–E refers to an injunction many chapters away from Exod 12:15; F–I refers to the verse

---

[20] My thanks to the Talmudic Studies Interest Group (Association for Jewish Studies, Dec., 1981) and in particular to Prof. David Goldenberg, President of Dropsie University. Their probing questions and advice led me to this formulation of matters. That they would all agree with this statement of the case, I hesitate to imply.

[21] Such results were found by Neusner in analyzing in particular how *Sifra* reworks passages of *mNeg.*; see J. Neusner, *Purities* VII (Leiden: Brill, 1975); see also notes 14 and 15.

subsequent to 12:15; and J–N, finally, highlights a disjunctive particle in 12:15 itself. The "wholistic" approach to Scripture, then, includes not only indicative or prescriptive statements but also formal, grammatical particles. Were this progression from rational exegeses to formalism evident in numerous pericopae, one could justifiably suspect a polemic against reason as such. But so to conclude on the basis of one example is premature.

I have argued that structure conveys meaning apart from the content at any one instance of the pattern. A brief discussion of the halakic substance of *Bo* 8 provides additional support for this assertion. The halakic aspects of the pericope seem innocuous at best. All three sections of the pericope agree that leaven is removed on the eve of the Passover. The alternative position, that leaven is eliminated on the 15th of Nisan, is a "straw man" throughout the passage. The halakic conclusion of the pericope is not particularly enlightening and only with difficulty can one imagine such an issue to be vital in the second or third century. There is good reason to suppose that at least within the Jerusalem Temple consensus on this issue had long been achieved. Since tannaitic *halakah* in matters pertaining to the Temple cult attempts to preserve and reappropriate—not criticize and redefine—that cultic law, post-70 rabbinism will hardly have debated the question in earnest. For the Mishnah's *Maseket Pesaḥim*, in any case, the removal of leaven on the eve of the Passover appears axiomatic; the tractate assumes it to be the case and nowhere debates the matter.[22] The halakic content of *Bo* 8 thus seems either trivial or beside the point. Unless we suppose the redactor of our pericope to be grossly ignorant of legal matters, the evidence strongly suggests that the editor's purpose is other than halakic instruction. That is to say, the midrashic process of the pericope, its structured pattern, bears the burden of the redactor's intended aims.

---

[22] Philo and Josephus, unfortunately, do not concern themselves with the issue. But the evidence from the Passover Epistle of the Elephantine Papyri indicates that centuries earlier the removal of leaven prior to sunset on the 14th of *Nisan* was accepted practice; see Aramaic Papyrus no. 21 (dated 419 B.C.E.) in A. Cowley ed., *Aramaic Papyri of the 5th C. BC* (Oxford: Clarendon, 1923), pp. 60–65; see especially lines 7–8.

CONTEMPORARY EXEGESIS
OF TALMUDIC LITERATURE
The Work of Shamma Friedman,
David Weiss Halivni, and Abraham Weiss

I. INTRODUCTION: METAPHOR AND EXEGESIS

Jacob Neusner
Brown University

ABSTRACT

A decisive element in the literary analysis of a text, particularly an ancient and unfamiliar one, is the metaphor chosen to describe the text and the method of its exegesis. The selected metaphor pre-figures the text and determines how it is read and the questions brought to it. Shamma Friedman's geological metaphor, which construes the Babylonian Talmud to be composed of layers or strata, is shown to be inappropriate to the text. The Talmud's own metaphor, that of *masseket* (the web of a loom), suggests a textured and integrated fabric of different strands of tradition and opens lines of inquiry more comprehensive and nuanced than those of Friedman.

The Babylonian Talmud (like Talmudic literature overall) is composite, a conglomerate of materials shaped under diverse auspices and at various times over half a millenium. Accordingly, one of the principal tasks of contemporary critical exegesis is to identify and describe the various components of the text as we have it. The purpose of such work is to explain how the Talmud was put together and what it was meant to say, prior to, and during, the stages in the process of agglutination or conglomeration. When the work succeeds, the result will be an account of the meanings of the text to the people who made it up. This meaning, we know, is distinct from its inherited and imputed meanings, based as they are on a unitary and harmonious reading of what, in fact, began as discrete and cacophonous. The consensus imposed through the labors of harmonizing redactors and commentators over a period of fifteen hundred years is to be replaced by a historically more congruent dissensus, exhibited to begin with by the constituents of the text.

In this labor of dissection and analysis, a principal problem is to find appropriate hermeneutical language, that is to say, metaphors for the exegetical labor. If we have no literary theory, generated by and expressed in metaphors, we can scarcely express ourselves intelligibly about the alien text. Through metaphors, we compare what we wish to explain to something we already understand. That is how we make sense of the unknown. Without metaphors, the alien text remains opaque, there being nothing to which to compare it. But the choice of the right metaphors is everything. As soon as we do have a theory of the text, embodied in usable metaphors ("this text is like . . ."), we discover that making sense of things in one way prevents our exploring a range of alternatives of literary structure and history. A striking illustration of the problem facing the contemporary, critical exegete of Talmudic literature comes to us in the deeply flawed, yet suggestive, work of Shamma Friedman, who is professor of Talmud at the Jerusalem campus of the Jewish Theological Seminary of America.

Friedman, whose work is laid forth extensively in the papers that follow, wishes to sort out the various components, or constituents, of the Babylonian Talmud. This he does by positing that they come into existence in three distinct and differentiable strata (or layers). Each of these strata is consistent within itself but different in form and conception from the others. The earliest stratum is made up of named sayings, the next, anonymous ones, and the final, other, yet later, anonymous additions. While making sense of what Friedman says is often not easy, because of his unselfconscious assertions that his most critical propositions require neither full and lucid articulation nor rigorous proof, we clearly see one thing. The operative metaphor throughout his work, defining the problems he will wish to take up and further govering the solutions he will propose, is inappropriate to his text.

Friedman's metaphor compares the Talmudic discussion to a composite of strata, three in all, one above the other. Whether or not a different metaphor will have led to the recognition of other problems than the one Friedman takes up can be determined only after precisely what he does is clear. Then, I believe, the reader will readily understand that Friedman defines as problems requiring exegetical solution aspects of the text to which his generative metaphor has drawn his attention. In several instances, if we did not know in advance (1) that the Talmudic passage is made up of distinct strata, named items early, unnamed ones later and (2) that the two strata exhibit differences of viewpoint from one another, we should not have known to ask the questions Friedman asks. What is treated as a problem in a fair number of instances thus becomes a problem only within the prior literary theory of strata, governing Friedman's reading of the text. And that prior literary theory is shaped by what I believe to be an inappropriate metaphor.

Let me now spell out this matter of finding appropriate metaphorical language for the formulation of the exegetical problem, explaining what I find wrong in Friedman's and proposing an alternative. (What I say here I pointed out in my *History of the Mishnaic Law of Purities* [Leiden, 1974], III, pp. 273-75.) Friedman's choice, as I said, is "stratum," with its corollary, "stratification." That metaphor, borrowed from geology, with some frequency finds its way into literary and historical inquiry. A stratum in geology is a bed of sedimentary rock, consisting of a series of layers. Stratification then is the formation of strata or layers, one above, and separate from, the other. Accordingly, the task before us is to uncover the several layers of the law. The problem with this commonplace metaphor is its stress on the distinctiveness of the several strata, their composing clearly separable layers of sediment. The inquiry into the nature of the stratification of the Mishnah or Talmud imposes the analogy of separate layers of accretion, agglutination, and development from lower (earlier) to upper (later). The discourse before us, however, is not illuminated by the metaphor of stratification, because it is far too closely interrelated. The metaphor rapidly is reified, so that it becomes natural to discuss the traits of a given stratum wholly apart from those of the next, as though the later one is apt to be unrelated, except through accretion, to the prior. This Friedman does throughout.

An alternative metaphor, "stages (of the law)," presents the same problem, for, while "stage" may refer to the division of a journey or process or a definite period in the development of a phenomenon, the more likely connotations are not much different from those of stratum and stratification.

The Talmudic tradition, by contrast, supplies an exact and intimate metaphor. Its title for a tractate of Mishnaic or Talmudic law is *masseket*. The word in Mishnaic sources refers to a web on a loom. In Amoraic times, and even more commonly in medieval midrashic compilations, the word is used as a metaphor for a tractate of the Mishnah-Talmud. What struck the Amoraim and later rabbis about the "web of a loom," and by extension, a piece of woven cloth, to draw their attention to its metaphorical values in describing a tractate of law? I think it was the recognition, made explicit in the earliest stages of Amoraic exegesis of the Mishnah, that any segment of the Mishnah and, we add, of the Talmud too, consists of a weaving together of many distinct strands of tradition, many threads composing a single, highly textured, whole and integrated fabric. That recognition is shown, for example, by the commonplace Amoraic inquiry, which we have continued in our own day, into the authorities standing behind anonymous statements of the law. The issue is, In accord with the established principle of which master does an unassigned tradition appear to unfold? Clearly, the Talmudic discourse weaves together many viewpoints, both on general principles and on specific issues. These viewpoints conceal still more subtle principles, in accord with which they are generated. So in using the metaphor of *masseket* the Amoraim seem to have meant, "a web of coherent law, part of a far larger fabric of law, itself composed of numerous individual strands of thread." (I do not mean to argue that other metaphors would not have served equally well. Presumably the importance of textile weaving in Babylonian Jewish communities gave the metaphor a certain resonance in the mind of the rabbinical circles.) The laws and discourse of the Talmud, viewed together, therefore are to be compared to fabric in the loom. Already woven materials are not before us. The threads of completed cloth at the bottom, however, are connected to what is woven but out of sight, so we shall be able to discern from the continuing warp and woof in the standing web the colors of the threads out of which the web has emerged.

While we have a considerable piece of woven cloth, we readily discern differences between what was woven earlier, at the bottom, and what was woven later on, at the top. These differences may be visualized as mixtures of different colors, created in the weaving together of various threads. At the bottom, the early part of the fabric, are primary colors, yellow, blue, red. These are woven together into brilliant and basic hues. If we then look upward, to the top, in the part of the fabric woven later on we see a quite different set of colors, though some threads of the primary colors still appear without sharing or muting. If at the bottom are yellow and red, toward the top we see orange. If a strand of the bottom is red and blue, toward the top we see violet. The primary bottom threads of yellow and blue yield green at the top. In between, toward the middle stages in the weaving of our fabric, the red and blue make magenta. Yet, if toward the bottom we see the primary colors, yellow, red, and blue, toward the middle, while these same colors predominate, the complementary hues emerge, leading naturally toward orange, violet, and green. Indeed, even near the bottom appears an occasional thread of green, just as near the top are yet the primary threads of blue or yellow, unmixed and still distinct.

The value of the metaphor is in helping to interpret the history of the discourse before us. The cloth is a complete Talmudic discussion viewed as a whole. The strands are main principles or themes of the law, which may well go from primary and unmixed, basic colors, to secondary and tertiary mixtures, obscuring the primary elements of which they are composed and turning the whole into an entirely new range of hues. Yet the whole is a single, well-connected, tightly woven fabric. That is the important point. No thread is lost. Nothing at the top is unconnected, either through the basic warp and woof, or through the insertion of a thread, skillfully and unobtrusively, into the standing fabric. Cut off the fabric at any given point and you will not omit a single major color, though some threads of secondary hues will be lost. At the end we shall return to our metaphor and describe what we may regard as the elemental colors, what are the secondary and complementary ones, and how the several threads are woven together.

The advantage of this metaphor of weaving, with attention to both the texture and the color of the threads, is that it allows for diverse relationships to be discerned among the constituents, or components, of a given discussion. True, it does not yield the satisfying result of Friedman's, that all named sayings belong in one category, all the unnamed ones in another (and this by definition!). It requires us to take seriously the layout of the text before us, prior to a dissection into predetermined parts, and to explain first what we have as a whole. Turning to the problems of formulation or interpretation generated within the metaphorical framework at hand is, properly, the second step.

The papers that follow on Friedman, prepared originally for a seminar in Talmudic exegesis at Brown University in 1981–82, Semester I, provide, first, an introduction to Friedman's fundamental propositions, and second, four examples of how Friedman deals with texts. The examples begin with a complete translation and exposition of the texts under discussion. They then provide an account of what Friedman thinks demands explanation and how he proposes to solve his problem. Finally, a brief criticism of his work is appended.

Our principal question is simple: (1) How does he know a problem is a problem? (2) How does he go about solving it? A reader with no prior knowledge of the Talmud should be able to follow the discussion. That, at any rate, is our intent. We deal with two further figures. One, David Weiss Halivni, also of the Jewish Theological Seminary of America, a professor of Talmud at its New York City campus, treats the same text as Friedman. This permits us to see how a prominent contemporary exegete takes up the same general range of texts. Halivni's success highlights Friedman's failure. The second, the late Abraham Weiss, was professor of Talmud at Yeshiva University. Weiss is shown to illustrate a completely different definition of the work of exegesis in our own day. The judgment of the seminar is that while Halivni and Weiss promise less, they deliver much more, and more credible, results than Friedman. This is because they allow the text to speak for itself—even (so to speak) when it stutters. Weiss's solutions, moreover, derive from concrete data of manuscripts, rather than convoluted exercises in merely-speculative reasoning. The fact that his exposition of his ideas is substantially easier to follow than Friedman's, I imagine, is no accident: clear thinking yields clear writing. Halivni is not second in these aspects.

The thesis of the seminar was that, if we can figure out why people know what questions to ask of a text, we can explain, also, how they form and produce answers. Friedman proved a serendipitous choice. Seeing how an infelicitous metaphor had distorted his vision, we were able to perceive rapidly and repeatedly why he produced results not much different, in fundamental logic and mode of inquiry, from those of the so-called "traditional" or pre-modern exegetes whom Friedman proposes, in method, to replace. *A priori* argument and deductive reasoning, after all, remain precisely what they are—even when garbed in Western clothing.

II. THE WORK OF SHAMMA FRIEDMAN

ABSTRACT

The papers in this section analyze the exegetical method of Shamma Friedman. Each examines in detail a segment of Friedman's long article, "A Critical Study of *Yevamot X* with a Methodological Introduction" (Hebrew), in H. Z. Dimitrovsky, ed., *Texts and Studies*, Analecta Judaica, Vol. I (New York, 1977), pp. 275–441.

Friedman holds that the Babylonian Talmud is composed of three literary strata. The first consists of sayings attributed to Amoraim (rabbis from the third through the early fifth century); the second comprises anonymous materials, lengthy legal deliberations on Amoraic sayings; the third is made up of late glosses to these earlier materials. Each strata, Friedman argues, is chronologically, linguistically, and stylistically distinct. The studies below assess the adequacy and utility of Friedman's theory and show, with textual illustrations, how Friedman's assumptions predetermine his conclusions.

i. Shamma Friedman's Methodological Principles

David Weiner
Yale University

In "A Critical Study of *Yevamot* X," Shamma Friedman develops an innovative approach to the study of the Babylonian Talmud. Friedman begins his work with a lengthy introduction, which sets forth his method of Talmudic exegesis. He then applies his method in a systematic analysis of b. Yebamot, Chapter Ten.

In the first part of his methodological introduction, Friedman relates his theory of the formation of the Babylonian Talmud, which provides the basis for his method of Talmudic exegesis. According to Friedman:

> ... from a chronological and literary perspective, we are able to discern three separate sources in the pericopae of the Babylonian Talmud:
>
> (1) Amoraic sayings
> (2) anonymous materials of the Talmud
> (3) late additions (p. 283)

The earliest stratum of the Talmud, in Friedman's opinion, consists of concise passages that record the views and actions of the early Amoraic authorities. This original layer was progressively corrupted by the insertion of later interpretations of the Amoraic sayings. These late interpretations were added to the text as part of a continuous process that began "in ancient times" and continued through the "post-Geonic period" (p. 287). Most of the materials that were added to the early Amoraic stratum are classified by Friedman as "the anonymous materials of the Talmud" (p. 283). These materials, which appear primarily in Aramaic, were formulated by anonymous editors. For the most part, Friedman says, this editorial layer consists of lengthy legal deliberations that augment and reinterpret the brief Amoraic sayings. In Friedman's view, the final layer of the Talmud is comprised of glosses tacked on to the text after the work of the anonymous editors was completed. In short, Friedman claims that it is possible to identify three chronological strata in the Babylonian Talmud, each with its own distinctive language and style.

Friedman's view of the Talmud's composition determines his program for modern Talmudic research. He maintains that contemporary studies of the Talmud must strive to delineate the chronological layers of the entire Talmudic text. Friedman anticipates that this process will yield important information for the literary, legal, and historical analysis of the Babylonian Talmud. The chronological division of the text will make it possible to trace the legal conceptions of the three generations of authorities which, in Friedman's opinion, stand behind the document. He writes:

> For the purposes of modern research, it is necessary to demarcate the chronological layers of all Talmudic pericopae, in order to examine the Amoraic sayings as a unique source, and to examine its distinctive form and content. Only in this way is it possible to study the origins of Talmudic law, i.e., the legal conceptions of the Amoraim in their own right, as distinguished from the views of those who formulated the anonymous materials which were tacked on to sayings of the Amoraim. Similarly, with regard to the literary analysis of the Talmud, the separation of Amoraic sayings from the anonymous materials of the Talmud will allow a thorough examination of the language, form, and literary style of each of these strata. (p. 289)

In addition to these long-term objectives, there are several immediate goals that, in Friedman's opinion, can be realized by distinguishing the various layers of the Talmud. First, it becomes possible to make sense of some unintelligible Talmudic periocopae. By separating the Amoraic lemmas from the anonymous discussions in which they are presently situated, we often find that what appears to be an unintelligible or illogical thread of discussion is actually a late interpretation added to an Amoraic saying by the redactor of the Talmud.

According to Friedman, the chronological division of the text will also result in immediate benefits for literary research. "The separation of the anonymous materials of the Talmud from the Amoraic sayings facilitates the work of identifying the structure of Talmudic pericopae, because the statements of the Amoraim comprise the foundation (i.e., the earliest stratum) of the Talmud, and these statements thus determine the structure of most Talmudic passages" (p. 316). Friedman thinks that once we have isolated the original building blocks used by the redactor of the Talmud, we can better analyze the principles that guided his construction of individual pericopae. In order to comprehend this subtle point, let us consider an example of the type of literary analysis proposed by Friedman.

Friedman considers cases (e.g., b. Yebamot 87b) in which an Amoraic saying is situated at the end of a long anonymous discussion. In these passages, the Amoraic saying often appears to be the final answer to a question dealt with throughout the preceding discussion. In Friedman's view, however, the Amoraic lemma derives from a period earlier than that of the rest of the discussion. It follows that the redactor of the Talmud began with an Amoraic saying, to which he added a long sequence of unattributed materials. Thus, Friedman maintains that his method can recover the process by which the text was constructed.

Friedman's research program has one further goal. The chronological delineation of the Talmud yields important results for comparative studies of the conceptions of Palestinian and Babylonian Amoraim. Isolating the statements of the early Babylonian Amoraim enables us to compare their views with those of their contemporaries in the Land of Israel. This procedure, says Friedman, generally reveals a striking correspondence between the legal theories of the Amoraim in the two distant communities.

In all, Friedman believes that delineating the strata of the text will illuminate many central issues of Talmudic research. First, the stratification of the Talmud will enable exegetes to elucidate many obscure pericopae. Second, it becomes possible to recover some of the principles that governed the redactor's construction of individual pericopae. Finally, the analysis of the chronological layers will ultimately lay the foundations for comprehensive examination of the history of ideas and expressions in the Talmud.

After presenting the basic goals of his work, Friedman confronts a crucial methodological problem: how to distinguish among the three chronological layers of the text. He claims that, for the most part, the task of separating the Amoraic sayings from the anonymous materials of the Talmud is "simple, obvious, and requires no substantiation" (p. 301). Any statement of the form "Rabbi x says: . . ." is deemed an Amoraic saying. In most pericopae, such statements are followed or preceded by long unattributed discussions. In these cases, Friedman simply assumes that the anonymous discussion is a late interpretation of the Amoraic saying.

In some instances, Friedman admits, it is rather more difficult to distinguish clearly the Amoraic sayings from the later anonymous additions. It is especially hard to isolate the editorial glosses that appear in the midst of Amoraic lemmas. Friedman, therefore, provides a list of criteria for differentiating the chronological layers of the text. These criteria are primarily useful for sifting out late interpolations that have been inserted into Amoraic sayings.

> (1) The statements of Amoraim tend to be brief, the anonymous framework in Aramaic. (2) An explanatory, dependent clause is usually editorial (i.e., from the anonymous materials of the Talmud). Further indications of anonymous "contamination" are (3) clumsy syntax, (4) excessive sentence length, and (5) resumptive repetition. (6) Material which when excluded from the passage leaves a simple, consistent text is likely to be an editorial addition. (7) References to

N. And if they died, a brother of this one and a brother of that perform the rite of ḥaliṣah but do not enter into levirate marriage.
O. R. Yosé says, "Her marriage-contract is [a lien] on the property of her first husband."
P. R. Eleazar says, "The first husband has a right to what she finds and to the fruit of her labor and to annul her vows."
Q. R. Simeon says, "Having sexual relations with her or performing a rite of ḥaliṣah with her on the part of the brother of the first husband exempts her co-wife [from levirate connection].
R. "And offspring from him is not a *mamzer*."
S. But if she should remarry without permission, [since the remarriage was an inadvertent transgression and null], she is permitted to return to him.

b. Yebamot 87b–88a

I. A. Since it is taught in the latter [portion of M. Yeb. 10:1], "If she should remarry without permission, she is permitted to return to him," [which means] without permission of the court, but rather on the testimony of witnesses, it follows that the former [portion of M. 10:1, which states that she may return to neither husband, refers to a case in which she remarried] with the permission of the court and on the testimony of a single witness. From this it is to be inferred that the testimony of a single witness is trustworthy.

B. And [in support of this conclusion] we also learned [in M. Yeb. 16:7], "They permitted women to remarry on the testimony of a second-hand witness, or on the testimony of a woman who reports the testimony of another woman, or on the testimony of a woman who reports the testimony of a male or female slave." From this is it to be inferred that the testimony of a single witness is trustworthy.

C. And [supplying further support for the same conclusion] we also learned [in M. Ker. 3:1], "If a single witness says, 'You have eaten forbidden fat (Lev 3:14–17),' and he says, 'I have not eaten such fat,' he is exempt from bringing a sin-offering." The reason is that he said, "I have not eaten," but if he remained silent, the witness is trusted. From this we may infer that the testimony of a single witness is trustworthy.

II. D. How do we know that this conclusion is derived from Scripture? For it is taught, ". . . or if his sin becomes known to him by a single witness, then he must bring a sin-offering (Lev 4:28)." This verse refers not only to a case in which others (plural) make his sin known to him. Going back to the case of M. Ker. 3:1, it might have been assumed that even if he does not deny it [the statement of the witness that he is eating forbidden fat], he remains exempt. The Torah therefore explicitly states, "If his sin becomes known to him," from any source, [even from one other person, he must bring a sin-offering].

E. How are we to interpret the foregoing proof? If one were to say that [it refers to a case in which] two witnesses [accused the man of eating forbidden fat] and he does not contradict them, why would I need a Scriptural passage [to prove the point? The testimony of two witnesses is always believed]. Rather, [the foregoing statement refers to a case in which] a single [witness accused the man of eating forbidden fat] and he did not contradict him [and the witness's testimony is trusted, so the man must bring a sin-offering]. Deduce from this that the testimony of a single witness is trustworthy.

F. But why [should we assume that his liability to bring a sin-offering] is because a single witness is trustworthy? Perhaps it is because the man remains silent, and silence is tantamount to an admission of guilt!

G. You know that this is the correct reason, for it is taught in the latter [part of M. Ker. 3:1], "If two people say, 'You have eaten forbidden fat,' and he says, 'I have not eaten it,' he is exempt [from a sin-offering]. R. Meir holds him liable to bring a sin-offering. Said R. Meir, 'This conclusion is based on an argument *a minori ad majus*. If two witnesses are sufficient to cause a man the severe penalty, death, should not their testimony be sufficient to cause a man to bring a minor penalty of a sin-offering?' [Surely, it is. Therefore, the testimony of two witnesses is believed and the man is held liable for eating forbidden fat and must bring a sin-offering].

They said to him, 'What if the man says he did it intentionally? [In this case he would not be liable to bring a sin-offering. The testimony of the witnesses in this case would have no effect. Meir's argument, then, that the testimony of the two witnesses is believed despite the man's denial, is not sound]."

H. Now in the earlier [part of M. Ker. 3:1] why do the rabbis hold the man liable [when one witness claims that he has eaten forbidden fat and he does not deny it]? If one says, it is because a single witness is believed, lo, with respect to a case involving two witnesses, who are always believed, even if the person accused contradicts them, the rabbis hold the man exempt [as in the passage of M. Ker. 3:1 cited above]. [Thus their ruling in the case involving a single witness is not because of his trustworthiness]. Rather, it is because [in this case] the man was silent, and silence is tantamount to an admission. [Thus the case presented in M. Ker. 3:1 fails to prove that the testimony of a single witness is trustworthy].

III. I. [Here begins a new attempt to demonstrate that the testimony of a single witness is trustworthy.] This is to be proven by logical argument. [The case of M. Yeb. 10:1] is analogous to the case of a piece which might be forbidden fat and might be permitted fat. [If] one witness comes and says, "I am sure that it is permitted fat," he is believed.

J. But is this really analogous? [No, for] there [in the case of the piece of fat], the prohibition [against eating this piece of fat] is not established [for it is the very nature of the fat which is in question], while here [in the case of a woman who remarries], the prohibition [against her having sexual relations with another man while she is still married to her first husband] is established [the question is only whether her first husband in fact has died and so whether she is permitted to remarry]. And cases regarding sexual relations are not established by less than two witnesses.

K. Rather is [the case of M. Yeb. 10:1] not analogous to a piece of fat which is definitely forbidden, [for in this case, if] a single witness comes and says, "I am certain that it is permitted," he is not trusted.

L. But is this really analogous? [No, for] there in the case of a piece of fat that is definitely forbidden, even if a hundred witnesses came [and testified to the contrary], they would not be believed. But here [in the case of M. Yeb. 10:1] since if two came they would be trusted, so too one witness should also be trusted.

M. Rather [the case of M. Yeb. 10:1] is analogous to that of *tebel* [= edible produce that is forbidden for consumption pending the separation of tithes or heave-offering], consecrated things, and *qonam* objects [= objects that are the subject of an oath and from which one may not derive benefit].

N. [We now take up each of these analogies in turn, demonstrating that they are not entirely adequate.] How does the case of *tebel* [demonstrate that a single witness is trustworthy]? If the produce is his own [i.e., that of the witness who claims that the tithes or heave-offering has been removed, then he is believed] because he has the power to effect the situation to which he testifies. But if the *tebel* belongs to another person, how does one reason [that the testimony of a single witness is trustworthy]? If one reasons that an individual may separate offerings from his neighbor's produce and does not need the permission of the owner, [then a single witness is believed] since he has the power to effect the situation to which he testifies. But if one reasons that an individual needs the permission of the owner of the produce, and a person says, "I know that he has separated the offerings properly," how do we know the principle [that the testimony of a single witness is trustworthy]? [We do not. Therefore, the analogy breaks down].

O. Likewise with the case of consecrated things. If [the case is of] the consecration of the value [of an object, then the witness who testifies that the object is deconsecrated is believed], for he has the power to redeem it himself. But if [the case refers to] an object which itself is consecrated [then how can we establish that the testimony of a single witness is trustworthy]? [For] if the object is his [= belongs to the witness who claims that it has been deconsecrated, then he is believed] because he has the power to cancel [his vow to consecrate the object]. But if the object belongs to someone else, and one [comes and] testifies "I know that its owner's vow has been cancelled." How do we know the principle [that the testimony of a single witness is trustworthy? Again, we do not].

P. Likewise in the case of *qonam* objects. If one reasons that the law of misappropriation applies to them, [then it is clear that the testimony of a single witness is believed], for he has the power to redeem the object. But if one reasons that the law of misappropriation does not apply to *qonam* objects and that it is merely the prohibition [against breaking a vow] that applies to him (lit., that rides on his shoulders), then, if the object belongs to the witness himself, [he is believed], for it is in his power to have his vow cancelled. But if [the object belongs to] another person and one says, "I know that its owner's vow has been cancelled," how do we know the principle [that the testimony of a single witness is trustworthy? We do not. This analogy, like those preceding it, is not acceptable].

IV. Q. Said R. Zeira, "Because of the hardships that are imposed on the woman in the end [if she remarries and then her first husband returns, the law] is lenient for her in the first place [permitting her to remarry on the evidence of only a single witness]."

R. One should be neither strict nor lenient.

S. The rabbis were lenient with her in order [to prevent her from becoming] an *agunah* [= a woman who cannot remarry because there is no testimony that her husband has died].

2. Outline of the Argument

I. Three cases which illustrate that the testimony of a single witness is trustworthy.
    A. M. Yeb. 10:1—the present case regarding a woman who remarries on testimony that her husband has died
    B. M. Yeb. 167—remarriage permitted on the basis of second-hand witnesses
    C. M. Ker. 3:1—a single witness who testifies that a man has eaten forbidden fat
II. Attempt to derive the principle that a single witness is trustworthy from the Scripture.
    D. The prooftext—Lev. 4:28
    E. The explanation and conclusion
    F. Refutation of the foregoing attempt
    G-H. Further support for this conclusion, i.e., expansion of this refutation on the basis of M. Ker. 3:1
III. Attempt to find a case analogous to that in which the testimony of a single witness is deemed trustworthy.
    I. Case of fat which might be forbidden and might be permitted
    J. Rejection of this analogy
    K. Opposite analogy is proposed—case of fat which is definitely prohibited
    L. Rejection of this analogy as well
    M. Three new analogies attempted and rejected: *tebel*, consecrated things and *qonam* objects
    N. Case of *tebel* considered and rejected
    O. Case of consecrated things considered and rejected
    P. Case of *qonam* objects
IV. A single witness is trustworthy at M. Yeb. 10:1 due to special circumstances of this case.
    Q. As leniency to balance the stringencies of law regarding woman who remarries
    R. Rejection of this principle
    S. As leniency to prevent a woman from becoming *agunah*

3. Summary and Critique

Friedman makes four observations about the text of b. Yeb. 87b–88a, which serve as the focus of his analysis. First, the pericope as a whole addresses a single topic: the reason for the principle, exemplified by M. Yeb. 10:1, that the testimony of a single witness may be trustworthy. Second, the pericope is composed of three separate literary units. Friedman delineates these in his outline, identical to the one presented above, except that he counts three units rather than four, since he does not label A–C as a separate unit. Third, he notes that the entire pericope is composed of anonymous materials, except the statement of R. Zeira (Q) (p. 324). Finally, he observes that units II and III begin with language (at D and I) indicating that their purpose is to discover the basis for the principle at hand. Unit IV, however, relates to neither of these units and does not carry forward this inquiry; it directly responds to the Mishnah.

Friedman states the essence of his comment clearly and concisely at the outset.

> From the perspective of chronology it is clear, according to our method, that R. Zeira's statement formed the original basis of the pericope and that all the anonymous material was added afterward as an introduction. In this way the pericope in its present form was created so that the words of R. Zeira appear to answer the question, "whence do we derive [the principle that the testimony of a single witness is trustworthy]?" at the beginning of the pericope; that is, they are presented as if they continued the discussion of the anonymous material. (p. 324)

In the remainder of his comment, Friedman spells out this claim about the literary history of our pericope. The anonymous materials of units II and III were not formulated in response to this Mishnah, but rather belonged originally in other contexts, b. Ker. 11a–12b and b. Git. 2b–3a respectively (pp. 326–8). This is clear, Friedman thinks, from the fact that they respond directly to the cases presented in those Mishnaic pericopae. In this context, by contrast, these materials bear little or no relation to the case at hand, M. Yeb. 10:1. The redactor of our pericope, then, has placed these units here specifically to make the statement of R. Zeira appear the correct and unchallenged conclusion to an extended discussion. As Friedman says, "Since at first the only words that referred to our Mishnah were those of R. Zeira, and parts I and II were added afterwards [parts II and III on our outline], it was necessary that these explanations be based on rejected interpretations, for the true answer was yet to come!" (p. 327). In short, in Friedman's view, the redactor began with the statement of R. Zeira. His intent was to demonstrate that this is the correct resolution of the issue posed by our Mishnah. He did this by borrowing essentially unrelated materials, which then could readily be refuted, leaving R. Zeira's statement at the conclusion.

Before proceeding to an analysis of Friedman's conclusions, it is important to notice precisely what questions his comment aims to answer. Friedman's analysis consists of two separate projects. First, he breaks apart a single pericope into its constituent literary units. Second, and more important, he presents an explanation of the redaction of these parts into their present form. That is, he claims to reconstruct the history of the text by presenting the principle(s) that governed its redaction. It should be noted that Friedman confines his comments to the redaction of the pericope as we have it. He does not discuss the composition of the individual units that comprise it. That is, he does not claim, in the case of b. Yeb. 87b–88a, that units II and III were composed at a later date than unit IV. Rather, his point is that unit IV was formulated in response to our Mishnah and is original to this context, while the other materials were placed here afterwards for a given purpose. Finally, it is important to recognize that Friedman is concerned only with the redaction of the text, not with the ideas expressed in it. He does not deal with the history of the law. He thus makes no effort to date either the principle that a single witness is trustworthy or the idea attributed to R. Zeira. He takes up only two tasks, consistent with the goals he enunciates in his methodological introduction. These are "to distinguish completely the statements of Amoraim from the anonymous materials of the Talmud so as to examine those amoraic statements in their own right," and "to analyze the literary structure of each pericope of Talmud."

It is apparent from the preceding summary that Friedman presents a plausible theory of the redaction of our pericope. He accounts for the striking literary features of the text. In particular, he explains both the inclusion of each unit within the text and the redactor's placement of each in its present location. To fully understand Friedman's work and the problems it poses, however, we must elaborate the assumptions that underlie his analysis. Some of these he states in his methodological introduction, but others emerge only from the substance of his comments.

Friedman assumes that the pericope under discussion is a unitary text. That is, he claims that it was constructed (in this case, from previously existing materials) by a single redactor for a single purpose, and that it was meant to be read as a continuous argument from beginning to end. There are grounds for this assertion. The connecting language at I is strong evidence that units II and III were meant to be read as a single ongoing discussion. The problem, as Friedman himself notes, is in the relation between units III and IV. He is careful to cite manuscript evidence in the notes to his outline indicating that R. Zeira's statement is to be preceded by the word, "rather..." This would provide a link between unit IV and all that precedes it, which is exactly what Friedman would like to demonstrate. But this conclusion is questionable, for the same evidence suggests an alternative explanation. R. Zeira's statement clearly is a separate unit from the anonymous material that precedes it, and the all-important connecting language is absent from standard printed editions of the Talmud. There is a possibility, then, that Unit IV is exactly what it appears to be—an independent ruling tacked on to the quite separate discussion in units II and III. Clearly, in the passage we confront distinct units that have been joined together. But this in itself does not definitively tell us either the chronological sequence or the purpose of their redaction.

Friedman makes another assumption that has broader implications for his method. He claims that Units II and III were originally formulated as commentaries to other pericopae of the Mishnah and were transferred to this pericope sometime later. He thus regards each unit of the Talmud as having been formulated as a commentary to some pericope of the Mishnah. This assumption, of course, is based on the literary characteristics of the Talmud as a whole. The Talmud, in its present form, is a discussion of and commentary to legal issues raised by the Mishnah. But when we analyze the distinct literary units that comprise the document, as Friedman does, this assumption may be unwarranted. Many sections of the Talmud appear to have been created as essays on a particular legal issue. Such self-contained units of law may or may not have been originally composed as commentary to the Mishnah. Moreover, even if we grant this claim, a further problem remains. Certain materials, like those in the pericope examined above, could have been created in response to several different Mishnah-pericopae. Friedman does not provide us with criteria for determining that a certain unit of the Talmud was originally intended to serve as commentary to one pericope of the Mishnah rather than to some other. The claims that the Talmud in every case presents commentary to the Mishnah and that we can determine to which pericope of the Mishnah it belongs can be proved, if at all, only by a careful analysis of each and every passage of the Talmud. It cannot be assumed prior to that analysis.

Friedman's most far-reaching methodological assumption, stated in the introduction to his article, is that anonymous materials should be construed as providing the context or setting for earlier amoraic sayings. This view underlies Friedman's claim that b. Yeb. 87b–88a was redacted around R. Zeira's statement, which alone was formulated in response to this Mishnah. But we could construct a quite different explanation of the redaction of our pericope. Units II and III could be seen as an essay on the issue raised by M. Yeb. 10:1. R. Zeira's statement could then be a late addition, redacted here as a solution to a yet unresolved issue. Admittedly, one must still account for the apparently poor quality of these attempts to derive the principle of a single witness from Scripture (unit II) and from logical inference (unit III). But it surely is not advisable to construct our theories of the text on the basis of what we think it should say, rather than to account for what the redactor in fact has created.

iii. Shamma Friedman on b. Yebamot 88a–b

Roger Brooks
Brown University

I take Friedman's comments on the pericope at b. Yebamot 88a–b as illustrative of his overall program of exegesis. To understand his method, it is necessary to know not only the sorts of questions he asks, but also why he asks them. Although I am interested in the answers Friedman gives to his questions, I prefer to know what, for him, constitutes a proper answer and solid evidence of proof. As earlier, this exercise begins with a translation of the text, followed by an outline, a summary of Friedman's comments, and a critique.

1. Translation of the Text

Mishnah 10:1
   A. The woman whose husband went overseas,
   B. and whom they came and told, "Your husband has died,"
   C. and who remarried,
   D. and whose husband afterward returned,
   E. goes forth from this one [i.e., the second husband] and from that one [i.e., the first].

b. Yebamot 88a–b

I.   A. Said Rab, "They taught [that the woman must leave both her first husband and her second husband] only with reference to a case in which she married [the second husband] on the basis of a single witness [who testified that her first husband was dead]. But if she married [the second husband] on the basis of two witnesses' [testimony], she need not leave."
   B. They laughed at this (so Friedman, p. 331, n. 2) in the West [i.e., in the Land of Israel, saying], "[Her first] husband comes [back], and stands [immediately in front of her], and yet you say that she does not leave [her second husband]?"
   C. [In support of Rab's statement, A, one may reply:] The objection [at B] in not necessary, [for we speak of a case in which] no one recognizes [the man who returned and claimed to be her first husband]. [Since no one knows this man, Rab is correct that the woman need not leave her second husband.]

D. [Rab's statement still is a problem, for] if [we speak of a case in which] no one recognizes [the man claiming to be the first husband], why [does Rab rule that the woman] does leave [both husbands, if she remarried on the basis of] one witness's [testimony]? [That is to say, since it cannot be established that the man who returned actually is the first husband, the woman need not leave her second husband under any circumstances. Rab rules, however, that she must leave her second husband if she remarried on the basis of one witness's testimony.]

E. [Again in support of Rab, one may reply]: The objection [at D] is not necessary, [for the case is as follows]: Two witnesses came [with the man who returned]. They testified, "We have been with this man from the time he left and until now. It is you who do not recognize him." [Thus it is established that the man who returned in fact is the first husband and, as Rab ruled, the woman does leave her second husband if she remarried on the basis of a single witness's testimony.]

F. [F and G do not advance the argument, but prove that it is possible for a person to go abroad and not be recognized when he returns.] For it is written [in Scripture], "And Joseph recognized his brothers, but they did not recognize him" [Gen 42:8].

G. Said Rab Hisda, "This teaches that the man left without any sign of a beard, and returned with a beard."

H. [We now return to the argument. Rab's opponents state that] the outcome [of the case at B–E] is that there are two [witnesses who state that the first husband is dead and that the woman is permitted to remarry], against two [witnesses who say that the first husband still is alive and that the woman should leave her second husband]. [The result is that no decision should be possible. Nevertheless, Rab contends that the woman need not leave her second husband.]

I. [The result of the problem spelled out at H is that] he who has intercourse with her [i.e., according to Rab, the second husband], is liable to bring a conditional guilt-offering, [for it cannot be determined whether or not a sin has been committed]. [Two witnesses testify that the first husband is alive, and that a transgression has occurred. Two other witnesses, however, state that the first husband is dead, and so no sin has taken place. Rab's ruling must be invalid, for it leads to this absurdity.]

J. Said Rab Sheshet, "[Rab's ruling does not create this problem, for we speak of] a case in which the woman married one of the witnesses [who testified that her first husband was dead].

[This witness knows whether or not he has sinned, for he knows whether or not his testimony was true. As a result, he need not bring a conditional guilt-offering.]"
K. [Rab's statement that the woman need not leave her second husband still is a problem.] [For even if the second husband is not liable to bring a conditional guild-offering], the woman herself is liable to bring a conditional guilt-offering. [She cannot know which pair of witnesses tells the truth, and so cannot verify whether or not she has sinned.]
L. [This problem created by Rab's ruling is solved if we refer to a case] in which [the woman] says, "It is clear to me [that the man who claims to be my first husband is not my first husband]." [Since she is certain that she has not sinned by remaining with the second husband, she need not bring a conditional guilt-offering. Rab's ruling therefore remains valid.]

II. A. If this is the case [that the woman is certain the man who claims to be her first husband is not her first husband], what purpose does [Rab's] statement [IA] serve? [That is, why does Rab restate the obvious, that the woman need not leave her second husband?]
B. Even R. Menahem b. R. Yose [who holds, as we shall see at C–D, that the woman must leave her second husband], refers only to a case in which the witnesses [who testify that the first husband still is alive] come forward first, and then the woman marries [a second husband, despite their testimony]. But if she marries [a second husband on the basis of witnesses who testify that her first husband is dead], and then [other] witnesses come forward [and state that her first husband still is alive, Menahem b. Yose holds that] she need not leave [her second husband]. [In cases of conflicting testimony, we maintain the *status quo*. The woman, therefore, remains with the second husband if she remarried before witnesses testified that her first husband still was alive. The question, then, is why Rab states what already is obvious, that the woman remains with her second husband.]
C. [C and D do not advance the argument, but present the source of Menahem b. Yose's position.] [His position] is in accordance with what is taught [at Babli Ketubot 22b and Babli Baba Batra 31b]: Two witnesses state that [her first husband is] dead, yet two state that he is not dead, [or] two witnesses state that she has been divorced, yet two state that she has not been divorced—lo, this woman may not marry [a second husband]. But if she does remarry, she need not leave [the second husband]. R. Menahem b. R. Yose says, "She must

leave [her second husband]."

D. Said R. Menahem b. R. Yose, "Under what circumstances do I rule that she must leave [her second husband]? [I say this] in a case in which witnesses come forward [and testify that her first husband still is alive], and then she goes and marries [a second husband, despite their testimony]. But if she married [a second husband, on the basis of witnesses who said that her first husband was dead], and then [other] witnesses come forward [and stated that her first husband still was alive]—lo, she need not leave [her second husband]."

E. [We now return to the question posed at the end of IIB, why Rab repeats an obvious rule.] [This repetition is not a problem], for Rab also [i.e., just like Menahem b. Yose] refers to a case in which the witnesses come first [testifying that the woman's first husband still is alive], and then the woman marries [a second husband]. [Rab rules that she does not separate from her second husband] to refute the opinion of R. Menahem b. R. Yose [who in this case rules that she must leave her second husband]. [Rab's rule does not repeat an established point of law, but has its own specific purpose. It therefore remains valid.]

F. Yet some say that the reason [Rab taught that the woman need not leave her second husband] is because she married [the second husband], and then witnesses came forward [to testify that her first husband still is alive]. [Rab's ruling then simply maintains the *status quo*.] But if witnesses had come forward [first, and testified that the first husband still was alive], and then the woman married [a second husband, Rab would have ruled that] she must separate [from her second husband].

G. According to whose [view is this latter interpretation, F]? It is in accordance with the position of R. Menahem b. R. Yose [spelled out above at IIB–D]. [The purpose of Rab's statement, then, is to reinforce Menahem b. Yose's ruling.]

III. A. Raba replied [the following to Rab's statement, IA]: "[Let us assume that the woman's second husband is a priest.] How do we know that if he does not wish [to follow the laws regarding forbidden marriages for the priesthood, Lev 21:1–8, and wishes to remain married to a woman whose first husband two witnesses had declared dead, but now two other witnesses declare to be alive], that we force [the priest to obey the laws, and to divorce her]?

B. "Scripture states, 'And you shall sanctify him' [Lev 21:8], even against his will.

C. "What case do we imagine? If you say that she did not marry one of her witnesses [who was a priest], nor did she state 'I am certain [that the man who claims to be my first husband is not my first husband],' would the statement that we force [the priest to divorce her] be necessary? [That is to say, if her marriage to the priest results in a liability to bring a conditional guilt-offering, it should be obvious that we do not allow the marriage to remain in effect.]

D. "[Since the statement that we force the priest not to marry her does occur], we must refer to a case in which the woman does marry one of her witnesses [who was a priest], and in which the woman states, 'I am certain [that the man who claims to be my first husband is not my first husband].' [That is, we must refer to a case in which it appears that the priest should be allowed to remain married to the woman, for the marriage does not result in a liability to bring a conditional guilt-offering.]

E. "[And from] the statement that we force [the priest, even though we might assume that the marriage is valid], we conclude that we take the woman away from him [i.e., make her leave the priest, her second husband]."

F. [The problem posed by Raba, IIA-E, then, is as follows: Although Lev 21:1-8 indicate that we cause the woman to leave her second husband if he is a priest, Rab, IA, rules that she need not leave him. To this problem, Rab may reply with one of the following three responses, F, G, or H]: (1) The prohibitions regarding the priesthood are different, [and Rab's ruling is not based upon them]. [While the woman might have to leave her husband if he is a priest, she need not leave if he is an ordinary Israelite. This is the case to which Rab refers, and so his ruling is valid.]

G. (2) Or if you wish, [Rab may reply]: What does [the statement that] we force [the priest] mean? [It means that] we force him by [close examination of] the witnesses. [That is to say, we require the court to search for witnesses whose testimony might disallow the marriage. If no such witnesses can be found, the marriage is permitted, and the woman need not leave the priest, as Rab rules (cf. Rashi, ad loc.).]

H. (3) Or if you wish, [Rab may reply]: [Lev 21:1-8] refer to a case in which] witnesses come forward [and testify that the first husband is alive], and then the woman marries [the priest]. [Because she remarried despite this earlier testimony, the woman must leave the priest. Rab's statement that the woman need not leave nonetheless is valid, for he refers to the

opposite case, in which the marriage takes place before witnesses testify that the first husband in fact is alive.]
  I. This [last explanation, H,] is the position of R. Menahem b. R. Yose [IIB–D].
IV. A. Rab Ashi says, "What is the meaning of Rab's statement [that if the woman married a second husband on the basis of two witnesses' testimony] 'She need not leave [IA]'? [It means that] she does not leave her initial permitted [status, i.e., she returns to her first husband].
    B. "And Rab previously has stated this! As it is taught [at Babli Yebamot 91a]: If the woman marries [a second husband] without the permission of a court, she is allowed to return [to her first husband] [Mishnah Yebamot 10:1S]. And Rab Huna quoted Rab, 'This is the law.'" [Since Ashi's interpretation of Rab's statement is consistent with another of Rab's rulings, Ashi's explanation is correct.]
    C. One statement is made by inference from the other.

2. Outline of the Argument

Mishnah 10:1A–E: A woman's husband has been declared dead. She remarries a second husband. If the first husband returns, she must leave both her first and her second husbands.

Rab [IA]: This rule applies only if the woman remarried on the strength of a single witness who testified that the first husband was dead. If she remarried on the strength of two witnesses' testimony, she need not leave.

  I. The Palestinian Rabbis object to Rab's ruling. He defends his rule by narrowing the circumstances to which it applies. This, in turn, draws another objection from the Palestinian Rabbis. This cycle continues through four exchanges:
    A. 1. Palestinian Rabbis [IB]: The first husband has returned, and now stands directly in front of the woman. How can Rab claim that she need not leave the second husband?
       2. Rab [IC]: The woman need not leave her second husband, for we speak of a case in which no one recognizes the man claiming to be the first husband. Rab's statement is valid, for it provides the proper rule in this case.
    B. 1. Palestinian Rabbis [ID]: Let us assume that no one recognizes the first husband. In a case in which the woman remarried on the basis of one witness's testimony, why does Rab rule that the woman must leave the second husband?

2. Rab [IE–G]: We assume that the first husband brings two witnesses who confirm his identity, and so the woman must leave her second husband. Again, Rab's statement provides the proper rule in this case, and so is valid.
   C. 1. Palestinian Rabbis [IH–I]: The result of Rab's supposition at B2 is that two witnesses confirm the identity of the first husband, while two other witnesses testify that the first husband is dead. The testimony therefore is inconclusive. This means that the second husband, with whom Rab says the woman should remain, becomes liable to bring a conditional guilt-offering when he has intercourse with her. This is because it cannot be determined whether or not the second husband has transgressed. Since Rab's ruling leads to this liability to offer a sacrifice, it must be invalid.
      2. Rab [IJ]: Let us assume that the second husband is one of the witnesses who testified that the first husband is dead. He knows whether or not he has sinned, and so need not bring a conditional guilt-offering. [Conditional guilt-offerings are brought only if the defendant is uncertain if he has sinned.] Rab's ruling still is valid, for no liability to bring a sacrifice is incurred through it.
   D. 1. Palestinian Rabbis [IK]: The woman herself cannot verify whether or not she has sinned, and so she must bring a conditional guilt-offering. Rab's ruling therefore must be invalid.
      2. Rab [IL]: We assume that the woman is certain that the man who has returned is not actually her first husband. The woman need not bring a conditional guilt-offering, for she is certain she has not sinned. Rab's ruling remains valid.
II. What purpose does Rab's ruling serve?
   A. It excludes the ruling of Menahem b. Yose [IIA–E]. Both Rab and Menahem b. Yose deal with a case in which the woman remarried after witnesses have testified that her first husband actually is alive. Rab states that the woman may remain with the second husband, in contradiction to Menahem b. Yose, who states that she must return to the first husband.
   B. It confirms Menahem b. Yose's position [IIF–G]. Both Menahem b. Yose and Rab treat a case in which the marriage occurs before witnesses testify that the first husband is alive. They agree that, in this case, the woman need not leave her second husband.
III. Raba presents a case in which Rab's ruling is improper: The woman marries a priest as her second husband. According to Lev

21:1-8, we should force the priest to divorce her, in order to preserve the sanctity of the priesthood. Rab's ruling that she may remain with the second husband, the priest, contradicts Scripture and so must be invalid [IIIA-E].
A. Rab may reply one of three answers:
1. Rab's ruling is based on practices for ordinary Israelites [IIIF]. Prohibitions regarding the priesthood, Lev 21:1-8, are more stringent.
2. According to Lev 21:1-8 we need not force the priest to divorce the woman [IIIG]. Rather we force him not to enter into a prohibited marriage. That is, before the marriage takes place, we carefully examine the witnesses who testify that the first husband is dead, to assure that they tell the truth.
3. Lev 21:1-8 implies that we force the priest to divorce the woman only in a case in which the marriage took place after witnesses already had testified that the first husband still was alive [IIIH-I]. Rab's ruling, however, deals with a case in which the marriage took place before the witnesses testified that the first husband in fact was alive. This is the position of Menahem b. Yose (see above, IIB-D).
IV. Ashi says that Rab's ruling, "She need not leave if she remarried on two witnesses' testimony," means that the woman need not leave her first husband [IVA].
A. This is in line with another ruling by Rab, from which it is stated by inference [IVB-C].

3. Summary and Critique

Friedman's goal is to compare what he deems to be two distinct types of sayings within the periocope. He distinguishes statements attributed to named authorities as one type, and anonymous sayings as another. To accomplish this division, Friedman removes the pericope's anonymous sayings, leaving behind amoraic ones. These amoraic materials, Friedman says, have their own meanings, independent of their present context. He claims that the meanings were changed when the amoraic sayings were combined with anonymous materials. For Friedman, the result of removing the unattributed sayings is to recover the original meanings of the Amoraim (pp. 283, 333). Friedman now has in hand what he supposes to be the original meaning of the amoraic material and the meaning imputed to it by the anonymous context. His substantive comments attempt to show that these are entirely distinct by demonstrating that each type of statement, amoraic and anonymous, treats M. 10:1 differently. Since the amoraic and anonymous sayings impute to the Mishnah different meanings, Friedman claims that they are distinct from each other.

With this outline of Friedman's goals and analysis behind us, let us turn to the details of his comments. Friedman begins by dividing the passage into three units (on our outline, I–II, III, IV). He says,

> The foundation of the passage is Rab's statement (IA), upon which are based three amoraic sayings. These sayings, together with the explanatory material following them, constitute the three sections of the pericope. Each of these stands independently, and is not connected to the others. (p. 332)

Solid evidence supports Friedman's claims. Each of the amoraic statements he identifies is interested in a different aspect of Rab's rule. As we recall, the first unit (I–II) treats the Palestinian rabbis' objection that the woman should return to her first husband. In the second section (III) Raba presents a case in which the woman remarries a priest, and so should not remain with him if the first husband returns. Finally, Ashi (IV) refers back to Rab's ruling and claims that Rab actually holds that the woman should return to her first husband. Friedman is justified in separating these three units, for indeed they take up distinct issues.

Friedman next turns to each of these units and attempts to isolate what he regards as its original amoraic statement (p. 333). Let us briefly summarize his results. The first unit (I–II) presents only one saying attributed to a named authority, Sheshet (IJ). Sheshet's lemma presents a problem for Friedman, for it is an integral part of the anonymous material that both precedes and follows it. This seems to disprove Friedman's notion that amoraic and anonymous statements are entirely unrelated. Friedman solves this problem by asserting that Sheshet's lemma does not belong in the present pericope, but has been moved here from b. Ketubot 22b. On the basis of this claim, he concludes that the entire first unit is anonymous, and contains no amoraic material at all (p. 333). We must note that Friedman's solution is completely unsubstantiated. It relies solely upon Albeck's comment, "It [i.e., Sheshet's lemma] has been moved here from Babli Ketubot 22b" (cf. *Tarbiz* 9, p. 170). Unfortunately, neither Albeck nor Friedman provides any evidence for this assertion. The second and third units (III, IV) present a different problem for Friedman's attempt to identify the amoraic material. In both cases, Friedman is faced with an amoraic statement followed by what appears to be explanatory (and anonymous) material. Friedman merely excises these explanations, leaving behind statements by Raba (IIIA–B) and by Ashi (IVA). He justifies this move by noting that explanatory materials mask the original meanings of the Amoraim (p. 333). But these explanations, as I shall suggest in my critique, are our only clue to the argument of the passage as a whole. Removing them ignores the Talmud as a coherent piece of literature. Within the entire pericope, then, Friedman isolates only two amoraic sayings, those of Raba and Ashi.

After identifying this amoraic material, Friedman poses two substantive questions: Do the Amoraim, Raba and Ashi, hold the same view of M. 10:1 as Rab? Do the anonymous sayings impute to the Mishnah a different meaning from the amoraic ones? Friedman claims that none of the Amoraim explicitly cites M. 10:1 as contradicting Rab. Since they are silent in this regard, Friedman reasons, they do not disagree with Rab's interpretation of the Mishnah (p. 335). He concludes therefore that all of the Amoraim, Rab included, hold a single view of the Mishnah. Furthermore, he claims that this "amoraic" interpretation of M. 10:1 is in sharp contrast to the view presented by the anonymous materials. In order better to understand these claims, let us spell out these two possible interpretations of M. 10:1.

Friedman claims that the amoraic materials present the same view of M. 10:1 as Rab. According to Friedman, Rab interprets the Mishnah's two cases as follows:

(1) A woman remarries on the basis of one witness and the permission of a court (M. 10:1A–R). When her first husband returns, she is married simultaneously to two men, and so must leave both.
(2) A woman remarries on the basis of one witness, but without the permission of a court (M. 10:1S). If the first husband returns, she must go back to him, for she never was validly married to the second.

For Rab, the difference between the two rulings turns only on the question of a court's permission. He assumes that in both cases the number of witnesses is the same (one). This, says Friedman, is the simplest possible interpretation of M. 10:1 (p. 283).

Friedman claims that the two amoraic sayings share Rab's interpretation of the Mishnah. With regard to Raba's lemma (IIIA–B) he says,

> Without the anonymous material (i.e., IIIC–E), Raba's question, derived from a *baraita* (Sifra Emor 1:13), is simple: "Rab has ruled that 'If she remarried on two witnesses' testimony, she need not leave her second husband,' even if she had remarried a priest. How can the court permit a priest to remain in such a marriage . . . , for the woman certainly is another man's wife . . . ?" (p. 334)

Friedman first notes that this *baraita* is completely unrelated to M. 10:1. Raba's question, then, deals only with a pericope in Sifra, not with the Mishnah. Friedman now mounts an argument from silence. Since Raba does not explicitly object to Rab's interpretation of M. 10:1, Friedman claims that these two Amoraim are in total agreement with regard to the

Mishnah (p. 333). Of course, this claim is weaker than it might be, for as Friedman himself agrees, Raba is not concerned with the Mishnah. Such an argument from silence would be effective only if Raba was dealing with M. 10:1 and still said nothing in contradiction to Rab's interpretation.

Ashi's statement (IV A) poses a greater problem for Friedman. Read in context, Ashi rules that the woman who remarried on two witnesses' testimony must return to her first husband. Rab, however, has stated that she need not leave her second husband. It appears, then, that Ashi and Rab explicitly differ in their interpretations of M. 10:1. As we recall, Friedman has already isolated Ashi's lemma from the explanatory material at IV B-C. He therefore turns away from this context, and focuses instead on the meaning of Ashi's statement, "she need not leave her initial permitted status." This same phrase occurs in two other passages, b. Yebamot 117b and b. Ketubot 23a. In those cases, Friedman says, its plain meaning is that the woman need not leave her second husband, whom she was initially given court permission to marry. On the basis of these passages, Friedman claims that Ashi and Rab agree in their interpretation of M. 10:1. Both rule that the woman need not leave her second husband. It appears that Friedman's argument here is sound. He quite reasonably expects Ashi's use of the phrase "her initial permitted status" to correspond to the Talmud's other uses of the same phrase.

We now turn to the interpretation of M. 10:1 presented in the anonymous materials. Unfortunately, Friedman never systematically deals with the anonymous statements within our passage. Instead he discusses the anonymous explanations of M. 10:1 contained in the previous pericope (b. Yebamot 87a-b; cf. pp. 323-30). This entails the assumption that the anonymous materials in both the previous passage and the present pericope make a single point. This assumption, it appears, is unsubstantiated by empirical study. Nevertheless, let me spell out the view Friedman imputes to the anonymous sayings. Once again I summarize the Mishnah's two cases:

> (1) A woman remarries on the basis of one witness's testimony and the permission of a court (M. 10:1A-R). When her first husband returns, she is married simultaneously to two men. This is not allowed, so the woman must leave both husbands.
>
> (2) A woman remarries on the basis of two witnesses' testimony. Since their testimony is deemed conclusive, the woman does not require a court's permission to remarry (M. 10:1S). When the first husband returns, the woman realizes that her second marriage was conducted in error. She validly is married only to the first husband, and therefore must return to him. (see b. Yebamot 87a; Friedman, p. 287)

Friedman states that the latter interpretation is "forced" (pp. 287, 335).

It reads into the second of the Mishnah's cases the complicating factor of two witnesses. The Mishnah itself never speaks of the number of witnesses involved in each case, but only of the court's giving permission.

According to Friedman, then, there are two possible interpretations of M. 10:1. The Amoraim uniformly hold the simplest view, while the anonymous statements represent a more complex interpretation. These two layers are substantively separate, just as Friedman wishes to prove (p. 283). But it appears that Friedman intends to justify a further claim, made in his methodological introduction:

> Viewed *chronologically*, ... we are able to distinguish three separate sources in pericopae in the Babylonian Talmud. These are:
> (1) amoraic sayings,
> (2) anonymous statements,
> (3) later additions. (p. 283; italics supplied)

His point is that the anonymous statements derive from later periods than do the amoraic ones because they are more complex.

Before turning to my critical comments, let us briefly review Friedman's analysis. He proposes to divide the passage into distinct layers, and then to place these layers in chronological order. He attempts to separate the pericope's amoraic materials from its anonymous ones and, on that basis, to argue that the two types of statements are substantively and temporally distinct from one another.

Friedman's entire project rests upon his separation of amoraic sayings from anonymous ones and thus his determination of the original meanings of amoraic statements. He believes that by so dividing the text he can recover an early (amoraic) stratum and a later (anonymous) one. This argument depends on the undemonstrated supposition that these two distinct layers, amoraic materials and anonymous explanatory statements, constitute historically separate strata. Friedman surely is correct that explanatory materials by definition are formulated in response to earlier rules. But, in itself, this claim is of limited significance for historical purposes. We know nothing of the span of time between the composition of the amoraic sayings and the formulation of their explanations. Such responses may have been composed five minutes or five hundred years after the statements of the Amoraim. Even if Friedman's division is correct at every point, therefore, he will have established nothing that might support any claim about the history of the text.

The basic assumption undergirding Friedman's historical claims is that simple ideas and interpretations precede complex ones. In his view, the amoraic sayings were formulated early because they impute to M. 10:1 a simple meaning. The anonymous materials offer a more complex view of the Mishnah, and thus derive from a later period. Two flaws diminish the effect and utility of this assumption. First, the categories of "simplicity" and "complexity" are undeniably subjective and, therefore, arbitrary. As tools of literary analysis, they are hopelessly imprecise. Second, Friedman merely imposes this evolutionary model on Talmudic texts. He supplies no argument for its superiority over other models, nor does he document its accuracy with rigorous demonstrations of literary dependency in particular cases. In the absence of such argumentation and demonstration, it is difficult to find compelling reasons to adopt his theory.

iv. Shamma Friedman on b. Yebamot 88b–89a

Judith Romney Wegner
Brown University

The fourth pericope of b. Yebamot, Chapter Ten discusses when and why a woman requires a writ of divorce from a "husband" to whom she is not validly married. The first part of the pericope (paragraphs A through G below) discusses two mishnaic rules:

(1) A supposed widow who consummates a marriage with a second "husband," and whose first husband later returns alive, is penalized: she must leave both men and must obtain a writ of divorce from both, thus losing her rights in both marriages (M. Yeb. 10:1);
(2) A supposed widow who becomes espoused to a second "husband," but discovers her mistake before consummation, is not penalized: she need not obtain a writ from the second "husband" and she may, moreover, return to the first husband (M. Yeb. 10:3).

The second part of the pericope (paragraphs H through K below) explains the reason why Mishnah Yebamot, Chapter Ten treats these two women differently, even though both have acted in good faith and both have made the same mistake. According to the *gemara*, the reason for the distinction is this: the first woman (in the case postulated in M. Yeb. 10:1 and the first clause of M. Yeb. 10:3) has violated a scriptural prohibition by consummating a second "marriage" while her first husband was still living; the second woman (in the case postulated in the final clause of M. Yeb. 10:3) has violated no scriptural prohibition, because her second "marriage" has not been consummated.

1. Translation of the Text

M. Yebamot 10:1

> The woman whose husband went overseas,
> and whom they came and told, "Your husband has died,"
> and who remarried,
> and whose husband thereafter returned,
> must leave both [the second "husband" and the first husband],
> and she requires a writ of divorce from both men. . . .

b. Yebamot 88b–89a

A. "She requires a writ from both men." Granted, she requires a writ from the first husband; but why [does she require one] from the second "husband" [also], this being merely a case of adultery [as opposed to a valid marriage]? [A wife who is divorced must, by scriptural law, be given a written statement to that effect, because Deut 24:1 expressly requires the husband to "write [a bill of divorcement] for her." In the case postulated by our Mishnah, the first husband must divorce his wife for her (albeit unintended) adultery. The question is, why must the second "husband" give a writ to a woman not validly married to him in the first place?]

B. [R. Huna answers the question posed at A, namely, why must the second "husband" give the woman a writ?]. R. Huna said: "[This is] a precautionary measure, lest people [wrongly] suppose that the first husband had [actually] divorced her and the second 'husband' had [validly] married her, and she [thus] appear to be a married woman leaving [her second husband] without [receiving] a writ [as required by Deut 24:1]."

C. [An objection is raised to R. Huna's answer at B, namely, that the writ from the second "husband" is required as a precaution, to obviate misunderstandings by people unacquainted with the facts.] But if so [i.e., if this is a precautionary measure], then [similarly] in the final clause [of M. Yeb. 10:3, cited below at b. Yeb. 92a], which teaches: "If they told her, 'Your husband has died,' and she then became espoused, and thereafter her husband returned, she is permitted to go back to him," might it not there too be [wrongly] supposed that her first husband had divorced her and the second had espoused her [i.e., the marriage was not yet consummated], and might she not [thus] appear to be an espoused wife leaving [her second husband] without [receiving] a writ? [R. Huna's explanation seems inadequate. He claims that the purpose of the writ from the second "husband" is to obviate misunderstandings. But if so, surely M. Yeb. 10:3 (just cited) would explicitly require the espoused "wife," whose first husband subsequently returns "from the dead," to obtain a writ from the second "husband" just as M. Yeb. 10:1 requires of the "wife" whose "marriage" has been consummated. Yet M. Yeb. 10:3 is silent on this point.]

D. [A solution is offered to the problem raised by C.] She requires a writ [from the second "husband"] in all circumstances [i.e., whether she had consummated as in M. Yeb. 10:1 or had merely become espoused as in the final clause of M. Yeb. 10:3, cited by C.] [D disposes of C's problem, by explaining that Huna would require a writ in the case of M. Yeb. 10:3 as well, even though the Mishnah

is silent on this point. Thus, Huna's explanation at B still stands.]
E. [An objection is raised to the solution offered by D.] But if so [i.e., if as D claims, a writ is required from the second "husband" whether the second "marriage" was consummated or not yet consummated, then a first husband could [mistakenly] appear to be taking back his [previously] divorced wife [following a subsequent marriage and divorce, in a case where she leaves the second "husband"] after she has merely been betrothed [to him]. [D has said that an espoused "wife," no less than a consummated "wife," requires a writ from the second "husband." This blurs the distinction between consummated and non-consummated marriage. Would it not follow that, even where the first man's wife was merely betrothed in error to the second "husband," she would require a writ from the latter before returning to the first husband? Then, if people mistakenly supposed that the first husband had initially divorced her, he would be suspected of taking back his divorced wife after a supervening marriage and divorce from a second husband (that is, of violating Deut 24:1–4).]
F. [An answer is given to the objection just spelled out at E.] [A man's taking back his divorced wife after she has become merely betrothed to another man is in order] according to R. Yose b. Kipper, who ruled [above, at b. Yeb. 11b] that "after consummation [with another man], she is forbidden [from remarriage to the first husband], but after mere betrothal [to another man] she is permitted [to be remarried to the first husband]." [R. Yose b. Kipper's ruling is explained at b. Yeb. 11b as based on the language of Deut 24:2. This forbids only a woman who has actually consummated with a second husband before the latter divorces her, to remarry a first husband who had previously divorced her. Hence, the concern expressed by E is misconceived. We need not worry that people may wrongly suspect a man of taking back his divorcee after a subsequent marriage and divorce, where the second man has merely betrothed her. For, even if the first husband had initially divorced his wife, R. Yose b. Kipper has ruled that she may remarry him in these circumstances. Hence, no precautionary writ is required here.] [Thus far, the *gemara* seems to have established the correctness of R. Huna's explanation at B. In the case of consummation, a writ is required from the second "husband" as a precaution to obviate invidious misunderstandings. We have further established that no precautionary writ is required in the case of mere betrothal with the second "husband." But the case of a mistaken espousal remains unsettled.]
G. [A new objection is raised to D's statement, that a woman who has espoused a second "husband" requires a writ from him, upon the

reappearance of the first husband, even though she may return to the first.] But from what is taught in the final clause [of M. Yeb. 10:3], that "even though the latter [the man who has mistakenly 'espoused' the supposed widow] gave her a writ, he has not [thereby] disqualified her from the priesthood" [i.e., from returning to a priestly husband, who by Lev 21:7 is barred from marriage with a divorcee], we infer that she does not require a writ [in the case of mistaken "espousal"; for if she did require a writ, how could this fail to disqualify her from [marriage with] the priesthood? [D had claimed that a woman who leaves a second "husband" after espousal, as in M. Yeb. 10:3, requires a writ, just as after consummation in M. Yeb. 10:1. But it is clear from the continuation of M. Yeb. 10:3, that this is not the case. Since a writ, even if given there, will not disqualify the woman from returning to her valid marriage with a priestly husband, we infer that the writ has no legal force. Hence a writ cannot be required in the case of mistaken espousal. D's claim is thus refuted.] [G has established that where a woman "remarries," mistakenly believing herself a widow, and her husband later returns, she requires a writ of divorce from the second "husband" only if the second "marriage" has actually been consummated. It is not required where the transaction has not gone beyond the stage of espousal.]

H. [H questions G's assumption that the author of M. Yeb. 10:3 was concerned with the requirement of a writ of divorce in a case of mistaken espousal. H assigns a different emphasis to M. Yeb. 10:3.] Rather, [in] the final clause [of M. Yeb. 10:3, just cited by G], they are saying that this was a mistaken espousal [and consequently the woman may return to her first husband (as was stated just prior to the cited language of M. Yeb. 10:3) even where the first husband was a priest]. [G had concluded that the reference to her returning to a priestly husband was made simply to indicate that no writ of divorce is required after a mistaken espousal. H now suggests a different emphasis. The sages were saying that, while a true divorcee may not be married to a priest, a "divorcee" from a second "husband" not validly espoused is not a true divorcee. She may, therefore, return to a priestly husband, even "writ in hand" if the second "husband" gave her one. The significant point addressed in M. Yeb. 10:3 was not whether a writ was required there. The rabbis were simply pointing out that the second "espousal" was invalid because contracted in error, and this is why the woman may return to her first husband. H does not, however, challenge the accuracy of G's conclusion that a writ of divorce is not required in the case of mistaken espousal. We have thus established that a writ is required from the second "husband" in the case of mistaken consummation; it is definitely not required in the case of mistaken betrothal; and apparently not required in the case of mistaken espousal. However, H has now shifted the focus of the discussion to other consequences flowing from the mistake in each case.]

I. [I raises an objection to H's interpretation of M. Yeb. 10:3.] [But, if the emphasis in the final clause of M. Yeb. 10:3 is on the mistakenness of the espousal] then in the first clause likewise, they are saying that was a case of mistaken consummation. [Yet] the rabbis penalized her [in that case, despite her mistake, in contrast to the woman mistakenly espoused in the final clause.] [The supposed widow, mistakenly espoused to a second man in the final clause of M. Yeb. 10:3, was not penalized for her mistake; the sages permitted her to return to her first husband—even where he was a priest. Yet the supposed widow, who through the same error mistakenly consummated with a second man in the first clause of M. Yeb. 10:3 is penalized. For the first clause says: "If they told her, 'Your husband has died' and she remarried, and thereafter they told her, 'He was alive [when you remarried] but is now dead,' she must leave [the second husband]." Thus, even though she is now in fact a widow and free to remarry, she was penalized by being forced to leave the second husband. In alluding to the discrepancy between the treatment of the two women in M. Yeb. 10:3, I is hinting that something else must be involved here, besides the mistake as to the first husband's death.]

J. [J spells out I's reasoning further.] [Moreover, since she was penalized in the first clause of M. Yeb. 10:3 despite her mistake,] in the final clause likewise they should have penalized her. [Since, in the first clause, she was penalized for the mistake as to her matrimonial status, why is the woman in the final clause not similarly penalized, seeing that she made the same mistake? Hence, there must be some other reason for the distinction between these two cases; and H must have been wrong to suppose that the crucial point in the final clause of M. Yeb. 10:3 was simply the mistake.]

K. [K answers the question posed by both I and J, by spelling out the crucial distinction between the two clauses of M. Yeb. 10:3.] [The difference is that] in the first clause, she had violated a scriptural prohibition, [and that is why] they penalized her; in the final clause, she had not violated a scriptural prohibition, so [there] the rabbis did not penalize her. [Scripture prohibits a woman from consummating a marriage with another man while her first husband remains alive and has not divorced her. Thus, the supposed widow in the first clause of M. Yeb. 10:3, who actually consummated with the second "husband," had (albeit unwittingly) violated a prohibition. In the final clause of M. Yeb. 10:3, by contrast, the supposed widow had merely espoused the second "husband." This did not violate the scriptural prohibition, since no consummation had occurred. Hence only the first woman, and not the second, had to be penalized. This explains why the first woman must leave her second "husband," even though her first husband is now certainly dead and she is theoretically free to marry the second man; while the second woman is permitted to go back to her first husband when he returns "from the dead."] [The pericope ends here, without either endorsing or rejecting R. Huna's original statement, that M. Yeb. 10:1 required the woman in that case to obtain a writ of divorce from a second "husband" married in error, as a precaution to clarify that she was not bound to the second "husband" in any way.]

2. Outline of the Argument

The pericope discusses when and why a woman in the circumstances postulated by M. Yebamot 10:1 requires a writ of divorce from a second "husband" to whom she was not validly married.

A. *She requires a writ from both men* (M. Yeb. 10:1). The gemara asks why a writ of divorce is required from the second "husband," to whom the woman was not validly married.

B. R. Huna states that it is a precaution, lest people wrongly think the woman was actually divorced by the first husband and thus validly married to the second man.

C. An objection is raised to B. If Huna is correct, what about the woman merely espoused to a second "husband" (i.e., where no consummation has taken place)?

D. A solution is offered. There is no problem; a writ of divorce is required in all circumstances.

E. An objection is raised to D. In that case, would not a writ be required even where the woman was merely betrothed to the second "husband"? If so, when she goes back to her real husband, he may appear to be taking back his divorced wife after another man has married and divorced her (and thus violating Deut 24:1-4).

F. An answer to E's objection. There is no problem; R. Yose b. Kipper ruled that a woman divorced by her first husband and then betrothed to a second man may be remarried to the first husband if the second transaction does not go beyond betrothal. (Thus it will not matter if people mistakenly assume such facts; so no precautionary writ is needed here.)

G. A new objection to D's statement that a writ is required in all circumstances. Is a writ really required even in the case of mistaken espousal, where no consummation has occurred? M. Yeb. 10:3

implies not, for it says that in such a case, a writ if given will lack legal force; it will not preclude the "divorcee" from returning to a first husband who is a priest (even though priests are barred from marriage with divorcees). This implies that no writ is needed in the case of mistaken espousal.

H. An objection to G. M. Yeb. 10:3 was not considering the need for a writ, but simply pointing out that while a true divorcee may not be married to a priest, a "divorcee" from a man not validly espoused is not a true divorcee. She may thus return even to a priestly husband after this mistake.

I. An objection to H. If the emphasis in the final clause of M. Yeb. 10:3 was on the mistaken "espousal," then the emphasis in the first clause was likewise on the mistaken "consummation." Yet the woman who "consummated" was penalized for her mistake (in contrast to the one mistakenly "espoused").

J. Support for I's objection. Since the mistake (belief in the first husband's death) was the same in both clauses, and the first woman was penalized but the second was not, M. Yeb. 10:3 must be concerned with something other than the mistake.

K. An answer to I and J. There is a crucial distinction between the two cases of M. Yeb. 10:3. The first woman violated a scriptural prohibition (by "consummating" with a second man while still married to a first husband). The second woman has not "consummated" her second "marriage"; thus she has committed no violation. Hence only the first woman was penalized. (The discussion ends without endorsing or rejecting Huna's statement that the writ from the second husband was required as a precaution.)

3. Summary and Critique

The main thesis of Friedman's analysis of b. Yebamot, Chapter Ten is this: in differentiating "layers" of talmudic material, there is a basic distinction between attributed ("amoraic") and unattributed ("anonymous") statements. Friedman believes that unattributed statements are generally later than those ascribed to named Amoraim; that is, he believes anonymous material to be the work of people closer to the period of redaction of the Babylonian Talmud. We have seen how Friedman supports this claim with respect to the first two pericopae of b. Yebamot, Chapter Ten. We shall now see how he justifies it for a third. A summary of Friedman's argument will be followed by a critique of his treatment of the pericope, both as a unit and in the general context of his method.

Summary

With the third pericope, Friedman uses a tool of analysis he has not previously employed; he presents a line-by-line comparison of the Babylonian pericope with its counterpart in the Jerusalem Talmud. He does so to show why the anonymous discussion in the third pericope *follows* the sole attributed amoraic statement rather than precedes it. This is necessary because Friedman has previously told us that "the usual way" of the Babylonian redactor is to insert his anonymous redactional material *before* an attributed ruling, to create the impression that this ruling is the culmination of a scholarly debate. By offering a plausible explanation for the unusual placement of the claimed redactional material in the third pericope, Friedman can maintain that the anonymous material here, as elsewhere, is the work of the redactor.

Friedman begins by noting that the sole attributed statement in the third pericope is Huna's lemma; all the rest is anonymous. Here, however, unlike the first pericope (where the sole attributed statement was preceded by anonymous discussion), the discussion follows Huna's lemma. This Friedman finds somewhat anomalous. Not only is it the reverse of the "usual" procedure, but also the "unusual" placement of the discussion results in unclarity about whether Huna's reasoning ultimately stands or falls. Huna's lemma concerned the mishnaic rule that a supposed widow, whose husband returns "from the dead" after her remarriage, must obtain a writ of divorce from her second "husband," even though not validly married to him. This, said Huna, is a precautionary rule, in case people wrongly suppose the woman's first husband had actually divorced her and she was validly married to the second man. As Friedman rightly notes, there is no obvious connection between Huna's lemma and the pericope's conclusion that the woman's liability to a penalty depends on whether the second "marriage" has been consummated or not.

After noting that the uncertain status of Huna's lemma bred controversy among mediaeval authorities, Friedman proceeds to explain the cause of the unclarity. He maintains that the entire Babylonian pericope, following Huna's lemma, was constructed by the redactor in deliberate conformity with the pattern of the corresponding Jerusalem pericope, which lay to hand. But, because the basic concern of the Babylonian redactor differed from that of the Palestinian rabbis, the redactor "expanded" the Jerusalem text by inserting additions to address the Babylonian concern while retaining the Jerusalem pericope's format. An unfortunate side-effect of this maneuver was to obscure the ultimate force of Huna's lemma.

To understand Friedman's analysis, we must adopt his format in setting the two pericopae side by side. (We retain Friedman's numbering of the Jerusalem statements, but employ the lettering used in our translation above to enumerate the Babylonian statements.)

Jerusalem Talmud	Babylonian Talmud
(opening statement by Samuel)	(opening statement by R. Huna)
I say that [we must allow for the possibility that] perhaps [her husband] had sent her a writ of divorce from overseas. [If so, she was validly married to the second man, and thus is barred from remarriage with the first by scriptural law.]	[This is] a precautionary measure, lest people [wrongly] suppose that the first husband had divorced her and the second had [validly] married her and she thus appear to be a married woman leaving [her second husband] without [receiving] a writ of divorce.

As Friedman points out, there is a basic difference in the problem addressed by the two pericopae. The Palestinian rabbis were worried by the possibility that the woman's missing husband had actually divorced her, in which case the second marriage was valid. If the second man now divorces her in compliance with the mishnaic rule, she will be barred by Deut 24:1–4 from remarrying the first husband, even though she has not, as the Mishnah contemplates, committed (unwittingly) adultery. The Babylonian authorities, by contrast, were concerned, not with the possibility that her husband had in fact divorced her, but with the possibility that people would wrongly suppose that he had. Therefore, Huna reasons that the Mishnah requires the divorce from the second "husband" as a precautionary measure, though not as a matter of law.

The two versions of the pericope then proceed respectively as follows (reproducing Friedman's parallel chart).

	Jerusalem Talmud		Babylonian Talmud
1(a)	R. Haggai objected before R. Zeira: But have we not learned, *If they told her, "Your husband has died," and she became espoused, and thereafter her husband returned, she is permitted to go back to him?*	C.	If so [if this is a precaution], then in the final clause, which teaches, *If they told her "Your husband has died," and she became espoused, and thereafter her husband returned, she is permitted to go back to him,*
(b)	But if you say [we must allow for the possibility that] perhaps he sent her a writ of divorce from overseas,		might it not there too be supposed that her first husband had divorced her, etc.?
	then let her be forbidden to go back to him.	D.	She requires a writ of divorce in all circumstances.
		E.	But if so, then a first husband could appear to be taking back his divorcee after she had merely been betrothed [to another].
2	But [in a case of espousal, as opposed to consummated marriage] we follow R. Yose b. Kipper, who ruled, "After mere betrothal [to another] she is permitted [to remarry her first husband, who had previously divorced her]."	F.	[This is in order] according to R. Yose b. Kipper, who ruled, "After consummation [with another], she is forbidden [to remarry the first husband who had previously divorced her], but after mere betrothal, she is permitted

[to remarry the first husband]."

3(a) But does not R. Yose b. Kipper concede that if the second husband gave her a writ, he has disqualified her from [marriage into] the priesthood? [i.e., does Yose's rule apply even where the first husband was a priest?]

3(b) [This is not a problem here, for] have we not learned, *Even though the second husband gave her a writ, he has not disqualified her from the priesthood?*

G. But from what is taught in the final clause, *Even though the second husband gave her a writ, he has not disqualified her from the priesthood,* we infer that she does not require a writ here; for if she required a writ, how could this fail to disqualify her from the priesthood?

H. Rather, in the final clause, they are saying that it was a mistaken espousal [and this is why she may return to her first husband].

I. Then in the first clause likewise, they are saying that this was a mistaken consummation. [Yet] the rabbis penalized her there [despite the mistake].

J. So in the final clause likewise, they should have penalized her.

4. The rabbis of Caesarea [said] in the name of R. Hela, "[The reason she requires a writ of divorce from the second husband is] to clarify the prohibition of the first husband [from taking her back in a case where she had actually consummated with the second]."

K. In the first clause, where she had violated a prohibition [by having intercourse with a man who was not her legal husband] they penalized her. In the final clause, since she had not violated a prohibition [being merely espoused to the second man], they did not penalize her.

Friedman makes much of the parallel structure of the two versions. Yet (apart from explaining the difference in the initial concerns of the two groups of authorities) he underplays the extent of the difference between the two pericopae. In particular, he fails to remark that the emphasis throughout the two pericopae is diametrically opposed. Since we shall return to this point in our critique of Friedman's analysis, we must spell it out in detail here.

The Jerusalem pericope, concerned as it is with the possibility that the woman was in fact validly married to the second man, emphasizes primarily the scriptural prohibition on her returning to the first husband after being divorced by the second. Indeed, the Palestinian rabbis' final conclusion is that the reason for requiring the writ of divorce from the second man is simply to clarify that the first husband is prohibited from taking her back in all circumstances; either because she is a divorcee from a second legitimate husband (Deut 24:1-4), or (if the first husband had not in fact divorced her) because she is technically (though unwittingly) an adulteress. For the Palestinian rabbis, the question of the mishnaic requirement of a writ of divorce from the second husband is secondary to the prohibition on her returning to her first husband. This is underscored by the fact that the mishnaic requirement is barely discussed (except to dismiss it as ineffective to disqualify the woman from remarrying a priest).

In the Babylonian pericope, by contrast, the concern is with the possibility of a mistaken assumption that the woman's first husband had divorced her. Here, then, the emphasis is reversed. That is, the required writ from the second "husband" becomes primary, while the question of the woman's returning to her first husband is secondary. Though the circumstances in which she may or may not return are noted, they are not disputed, since all accept R. Yose b. Kipper's ruling on the point. The main thrust of the Babylonian discussion is to explain that the writ from the second "husband" is needed, not because she must leave him (though all agree that she must, since M. Yeb. 10:1 says so), but to clarify any possible confusion as to whether she is legally bound to him.

What emerges, then, is that two completely different, self-contained discussions are built around appeals to the same three authorities in each case (two mishnaic rules, at 1a = C and 3b = G, and one tannaitic ruling, at 2 = F). Yet Friedman downplays the differences by not analyzing them in detail as we have done here. Instead, he concentrates on the asserted "parallelism." He claims that the extensiveness of the "parallels" proves that the Babylonian pericope is the work of a single redactor, who modeled it consciously on the Jerusalem pericope, which lay to hand. The discrepant additions, he says, result from the redactor's attempt to fit the quite different Babylonian concerns to the Jerusalem format. That is to say, the redactor took a pericope that dealt with the problem of preventing a woman's return to a husband from whom she was barred by law, and reworked it to fit the problem of avoiding a mistaken assumption that a married woman had left her husband without receiving a bill of divorce. But the redactor's insistence on preserving the Jerusalem format forced the placing of the anonymous discussion after Huna's lemma, rather than before it in the more usual fashion. With this explanation, Friedman rebuts in advance an anticipated criticism, namely, that this unusual placement of anonymous material precludes his claiming, in this instance, that the material was inserted by the redactor. Moreover, says Friedman, his explanation accounts also for the obscuring of the ultimate force of Huna's lemma mentioned above. On the one hand, the fact that the conclusion of the intervening discussion has no connection with Huna's lemma makes this appear to have been rejected. On the other hand, the fact that the discussion is entirely unattributed makes

Huna's reasoning appear to stand, inasmuch as no named authority has refuted it.

Critique

In his treatment of the fourth pericope, Friedman continues to propound his thesis that unattributed material in the Babylonian Talmud is distinct from and later than attributed amoraic statements. Yet the impression persists that this "hypothesis" is in fact an *a priori* conclusion that he is determined to maintain at any cost. In fact b. Yebamot, Chapter Ten exhibits no single consistent criterion, or set of criteria, which demonstrates Friedman's asserted dichotomy between attributed and unattributed material. Friedman is thus forced to resort to *ad hoc* arguments from one pericope to the next.

In the first pericope (discussed by Newman above), the "anonymous" material (consisting of items which, so Friedman claims, were transferred from original locations elsewhere) appears in the text before the sole attributed statement, a comment by Zeira. Despite this order of placement, Friedman argued that Zeira's statement antedated the rest of the pericope and the redactor placed the anonymous material first so as to create a "build-up" for that statement. The latter thus appears as the final, agreed conclusion of a lengthy scholarly debate. This device, says Friedman, is a frequent phenomenon in the Babylonian Talmud and a sure sign of redactional activity. Here, Friedman's argument for separate provenance of the anonymous material was quite convincing, since Zeira's statement directly addressed the problem raised in the Mishnah, while the rest of the discussion did not. But the mere fact that anonymous material is of distinct provenance does not necessarily prove that it is later rather than earlier. Nor does it prove that all was the work of a single author, namely the redactor.

In the second pericope (discussed by Brooks above), Friedman showed that all the anonymous material in fact emanated from various other talmudic locations, and he gave several "proofs" that the unattributed statements were later than those attributed to named authorities. However, he was not able to demonstrate that all the disparate fragments were transferred by the same hand, or at the same time. Nor could he show precisely when this occurred; in particular, he did not substantiate his claim that all was the work of a single, final redactor.

We turn now to the third pericope. Here, we find Friedman's *a priori* assumption (that "anonymous" equals "redactional") once more called into question by flaws in his method. As before, he must confront the problem that there is no single, consistent criterion (such as use of language, or style of argument) to which he can point throughout the tractate, or even throughout the chapter viewed as a separate unit. Thus, he is once more forced to look for *ad hoc* evidence to support his preconceived conclusion. In the case of the fourth pericope, Friedman finds this evidence in a striking "parallelism" which he discerns between the Babylonian and Jerusalem versions of the pericope.

Unfortunately, there are several problems in Friedman's presentation of the material. On the one hand, he sometimes ignores the possibility of alternative explanations of the data in question. On the other, he fails to take maximum advantage of some points which would actually support his hypothesis. We shall consider both these aspects of his handling of the "parallel" he perceives between the two versions of the pericope.

As his chart shows, Friedman's evidence for the parallel consists of the fact that both versions invoke the same three authorities: the two mishnaic rulings from M. Yeb. 10:3, and the ruling of Yose b. Kipper, as noted above. But Friedman's argument ignores that fact that, as both versions are discussing the same Mishnah (*She requires a writ of divorce from both men*), is is hardly surprising that they appeal to the same authorities. What other choice, we may ask, did the disputants have in either case? Clearly, the same authorities are equally in point for both discussions. It is true that these authorities are adduced in the development of two different opening statements (Samuel's on the one hand and Huna's on the other), which emphasize two different aspects of the problem. Yet since the basic subject matter is the same, and since the cited mishnaic authorities play a logical part in the development of both arguments, it is quite possible that these "parallels" occurred in the natural course of events. That is, the "parallelism" could be as well explained by the fact that both groups of rabbis are discussing the same mishnaic rule (M. Yeb. 10:1), as by the deliberate modeling of one pericope upon the other alleged by Friedman.

Thus, on the one hand, Friedman may be reading too much into the invocation of the same three authorities in both versions. On the other hand, he fails to derive maximum advantage from his own argument. For instance, he could have strengthened his hand by pointing out that the three citations appear in the same order in both versions, even though they are cited for quite different purposes. (While this is perhaps implicit in his spacing of the chart, he does not mention it explicitly.) Again, while relying heavily on the formal parallelism, Friedman pays insufficient attention to the actual content of the two versions. It is a curious fact that, though the form may be parallel, the content is in effect reversed. The Jerusalem pericope opens with a discussion of the need to penalize the woman and closes with an explanation of the required writ of divorce from the second man. The Babylonian pericope opens with an explanation of the required writ of divorce from the second man and closes with a discussion of the need to penalize the woman.

Friedman fails to discuss the relevance to his theory of this reversal of content in a pericope of assertedly parallel construction. This failure is surprising; the data here might be thought to strengthen his hypothesis in that the redactor's "fabrication" could thus be presented as an even more impressive *tour de force*. Had Friedman made the points just noted, his parallel presentation of the two pericopae might seem less Procrustean. As it is, we are struck mainly by the extent to which he had to "stretch out" the Jerusalem version, opposing large gaps to the alleged "additions" in the Babylonian version, in order to place each Babylonian appeal to authority parallel to its Jerusalem counterpart.

Perhaps the strongest point in Friedman's argument is this: the net effect of the Babylonian discussion, as he points out, is to obscure the ultimate force of Huna's statement, that the writ of divorce required from the second "husband" is a precautionary measure. If we have before us a more or less faithful record of an actual discussion, it is surprising that that discussion does not end by either endorsing or rejecting Huna's reasoning. This anomaly could indeed have resulted, as Friedman claims, from a redactor's attempt to construct a parallel pericope. For, in order to retain the Jerusalem format, the Babylonian redactor would have had to place Huna's lemma precisely where it appears, at the head of the pericope, so as to match its position to Samuel's lemma in the Jerusalem version. But if so, Huna's lemma could not be placed last, so as to appear (like Zeira's in the first pericope) as an agreed conclusion to the discussion; hence the ambiguity, discussed above, on whether Huna's statement was ultimately accepted or rejected. Yet, instead of stressing this good substantive argument for a spurious pericope, Friedman concentrates on the formal rather than the substantive aspect. The formal problem lies in the very fact that we have here a reversal of the "usual" order. On Friedman's own theory, attributed statements should appear after anonymous, redactional material, and not before. So, in pressing his claim that the anonymous material here, as elsewhere, is redactional, he thinks that his main problem is to account for the reversed order.

Here, Friedman's method seems to exhibit a serious weakness. In explaining the reversal of the material, he begs the whole question of redactional provenance, and commits a *non sequitur* besides. Both fallacies are inherent in his reasoning, whose steps are as follows: (1) Friedman posits that anonymous material in the Babylonian Talmud is redactional. (2) One indicator is its usual placement as an introduction to an attributed amoraic statement. (3) In the present case, Friedman can plausibly account for the reversal of the usual order as resulting from the desire to fabricate a parallel pericope. (4) Therefore, this pericope can be treated as though the anonymous material appeared in its usual position. (5) Hence, it is not "disqualified" from being redactional. (6) Therefore, it is the work of the redactor.

There are two fallacies here. One is the *petitio principii*: Friedman begins by assuming what he then sets out to prove. The other is the *non sequitur*: by demonstrating that the reversal of the usual order need not preclude a claim that the pericope is redactional, Friedman seems to think he has effectively proved that it is indeed the work of the redactor. Yet the evidence in the third pericope is at best equivocal. Suppose, for instance, we grant that Friedman has demonstrated convincingly that someone deliberately constructed a parallel pericope. It does not necessarily follow that that someone was a late, final redactor. The pericope could have been produced at any time after the time of the authorities named in the two pericopes. Huna was a fourth-generation Amora, who spent time in both Palestine and Babylon. He was a contemporary fo the Haggai mentioned in the Jerusalem pericope; both lived in the early fourth century. Who is to say that the "spurious" Babylonian pericope was not composed by the school of Huna and passed on as tradition until its ultimate incorporation by the Babylonian redactor?

Friedman's general methodological error is this. Though all redactional material is, virtually by definition, anonymous, it cannot be assumed that all anonymous material is redactional. Anonymous material is simply an eligible candidate for consideration as to its redactional character. Such a conclusion, however, must be based on arguments beyond the mere fact of anonymity. Unfortunately, if there is some characteristic or set of characteristics which can reliably identify all redactional material in the Babylonian Talmud, Friedman does not seem to have found it. He therefore has to treat each pericope on an *ad hoc* basis. The most that can be offered in each case, then, is a more or less plausible argument that the material in question may be redactional. But there is often some other, equally plausible interpretation. Friedman may well be right in most, if not all, of his identifications of redactional material in b. Yebamot, Chapter Ten. Unfortunately, his hypothesis that "anonymous" equals "redactional" is capable neither of verification nor of falsification by the *ad hoc* methods he employs; nor, perhaps, by any means at all.

III. THE WORK OF DAVID WEISS HALIVNI
A Source-Critical Commentary to b. Yebamot 87b

Louis Newman
Carleton College

ABSTRACT

David Weiss Halivni divides the Babylonian Talmud into two types of material: "sources" and "traditions." "Sources" are materials that appear in the Talmud in their original form. "Traditions" are materials that have been altered in the course of transmission. By directing his attention to forced Talmudic interpretations of the Mishnah, Halivni is able to distinguish "sources" from "traditions." His method stresses careful attention to literal connotations and straightforward meanings of Talmudic literature.

My purpose in this essay is to present the exegetical program of David Weiss Halivni and to compare it with that of Shamma Friedman. To accomplish this, I review Halivni's comments to b. Yeb. 87b, a passage of Talmud analyzed in detail by Friedman. These two Talmudic scholars approach the text with widely divergent goals. Halivni's exegesis proceeds inductively. He locates difficult passages within the text and draws on further textual evidence to resolve those difficulties. Friedman, by contrast, approaches the Talmud with a pre-established theory of the text and its history. The exegetical insights of his analysis are secondary to the hypotheses he wishes to test. By juxtaposing the two, I hope to illustrate the diversity of methods employed in the modern, critical exegesis of the Talmud and so highlight the significance of the choices that each of these exegetes has made.

The foundation of Halivni's exegetical method is his distinction between what he terms "sources" and "traditions." In Halivni's words, "We call 'sources' those statements that we have in their original form, as they were uttered by their authors. Those statements that were altered in the course of their transmission, we call 'traditions.'"[1] Underlying this distinction is Halivni's fundamental conception of the development of the Babylonian Talmud. Halivni believes that many early rabbinic statements ("sources") became corrupted during a lengthy period of oral transmission. This posed a problem for later rabbinic authorities who attempted to make sense of these materials. The Amoraim of a later period often found it difficult to reconcile versions of earlier sayings that Halivni regards as corrupt ("traditions") with other rulings that Halivni believes had been transmitted correctly. As a result, these authorities often resorted to forced interpretations in order to make sense of the materials before them.[2] Halivni wishes to distinguish these forced interpretations from simple ones. The simplest reading of a passage, for Halivni, is the one "that arises from the text itself, without either adding to it or subtracting from it."[3] A forced interpretation, by contrast, is one that rejects the plain meaning of a passage. Interpretations of this type constitute the problematic of Halivni's exegesis. They alert him to the possibility that a source was distorted during its transmission to later Amoraim. The primary goal of Halivni's work, then, is to recover the "source," that is, the original form of the statement in question. His task as an exegete is to solve "the problem of forced interpretations," which, he claims, is "the fundamental problem of research on the Babylonian Talmud."[4]

Let us briefly examine how Halivni proposes to recover the original "sources" lost to later generations of Amoraim. For the most part, he solves the textual problems he encounters by drawing upon other rabbinic texts. For example, he refers frequently to passages in the Palestinian Talmud and in Tosefta that parallel pericopae in the Babylonian Talmud. He also turns to manuscript evidence and to Geonic literature in his attempt to reconstruct the original form of a Talmudic source. In some cases, textual evidence of this sort is either unavailable or unhelpful. Under these circumstances, Halivni pursues a close reading of the passage in question as it appears in the printed edition of the Talmud. This, he hopes, will lead him to recover the original meaning of the text, which had eluded the Amoraim. The primary resources of Halivni's exegesis are parallel sources and textual variants.[5] His goal is to recover

---

[1] David Weiss Halivni, *Sources and Traditions: A Source Critical Commentary on Seder Nashim* (Tel Aviv: Dvir, 1968), p. 7, note 1.
[2] See Halivni's discussion of other sources of forced interpretations, ibid., pp. 13–17.
[3] Ibid., p. 8.
[4] Ibid., p. 14.
[5] See David Goodblatt, "David Weiss Halivni: *Meqorot Umesorot*: Gittin" in Jacob Neusner, ed., *Formation of the Babylonian Talmud* (Leiden: E. J. Brill, 1973). See especially p. 165, note 6 where Goodblatt attempts a rough classification of Halivni's comments according to the method of exegesis which Halivni employs.

the "sources" of each passage he considers from within the corpus of rabbinic literature itself.

Let us turn now to Halivni's comments on b. Yeb. 87b, which follow a clear, logical order. He begins by focusing on the Talmud's interpretation of M. Yeb. 10:1. The Talmud's reading of the Mishnah clearly is forced, and this signals to Halivni the presence of an exegetical difficulty. The forced reading leads Halivni to believe that the Amoraim may have misunderstood the original meaning of the Mishnah. After considering alternative readings of M. Yeb. 10:1, Halivni concludes by offering his own interpretation, which, he believes, better conforms to the language of the pericope and avoids the problems inherent in other possible interpretations.

The following summary of Halivni's comments presents the texts he examines, M. Yeb. 10:1 and the beginning of the Talmud's discussion of it, at b. Yeb. 87b.

Mishnah 10:1   A. The woman whose husband went overseas,
B. and whom they came and told, "Your husband has died,"
C. and who remarried,
D. and whose husband afterward returned,
E. (1) goes forth from this one [the second husband] and from that one [the first].
F. And (2) she requires a writ of divorce from this one and from that.
G. And she has no claim of (3) [payment of her] marriage-contract, (4) of usufruct, (5) of alimony, or (6) of indemnification, either on this one or on that.
H. (7) If she had collected anything [of G] from this one or from that, she must return it.
I. (8) And the offspring is deemed a *mamzer*, whether born of the one marriage or the other.
J. And (9) neither one of them [if he is a priest] becomes unclean for her [if she should die and require burial].
K. And neither one of them has the right either (10) to what she finds or (11) to the fruit of her labor, or (12) to annul her vows.
L. [If] (13) she was an Israelite girl, she is rendered invalid for marriage into the priesthood; a Levite, from eating tithe; and a priest-girl, from eating heave-offering.
M. And the heirs of either one of the husbands do not inherit her *ketubah*.
N. And if they died, a brother of this one and a brother of that perform the rite of *ḥaliṣah* but do not enter into levirate marriage.
O. R. Yosé says, "Her marriage-contract is [a lien] on the

property of her first husband."
P. R. Eleazar says, "The first husband has a right to what she finds and to the fruit of her labor and to annul her vows."
Q. R. Simeon says, "Having sexual relations with her or performing a rite of ḥaliṣah with her on the part of the brother of the first husband exempts her co-wife [from levirate connection].
R. "And offspring from him is not a *mamzer*."
S. But if she should remarry without permission, [since the remarriage was an inadvertant transgression and null], she is permitted to return to him.

b. Yeb. 87b

I. A. Since it is taught in the latter [portion of M. Yeb. 10:1], "If she should remarry without permission, she is permitted to return to him," [which means] without permission of the court, but rather on the testimony of witnesses, it follows that the former [portion of M. 10:1 which states that she may return to neither husband refers to a case in which she remarried] with the permission of the court and on the testimony of a single witness. From this it is to be inferred that the testimony of a single witness is trustworthy.

B. [In support of this conclusion] And we also learned [in M. Yeb 16:7], "They permitted women to remarry on the testimony of a second-hand witness, or on the testimony of a woman who reports the testimony of another woman, or on the testimony of a woman who reports the testimony of a male or female slave." From this it is to be inferred that the testimony of a single witness is trustworthy.

C. [Supplying further support for the same conclusion] And we also learned [in M. Keritot 3:1], "If a single witness says, 'You have eaten forbidden fat (Lev 3:14-17),' and he says, 'I have not eaten such fat,' he is exempt from bringing a sin-offering." The reason is that he said, "I have not eaten," but if he remained silent, the witness is trusted. From this we may infer that the testimony of a single witness is trustworthy.

Reviewing the texts before us, we notice that M. Yeb. 10:1 presents two distinct cases. The first, at A–N+0–R, concerns a woman who hears that her husband has died and subsequently remarries. When her first husband returns, she is treated as an adultress. She therefore is required to leave both men and receives none of the benefits to which she would ordinarily be entitled under either marriage. The second case, at S, considers a woman who remarries "without permission." Since this woman's action was not authorized, her second marriage was never valid. She thus is permitted to return to her first husband when he reappears. The Talmud opens its discussion of this pericope by introducing a distinction between the two cases that is not found in the Mishnah (I A). According to the Talmud, the woman referred to at A–R remarried on the testimony of a single witness, while the woman mentioned at S relied on the testimony of two witnesses. A lengthy discussion follows (beginning at I B–C), in which the Talmud attempts to locate the basis of the principle that a single witness who testifies on matters of a woman's status is trustworthy.

Halivni's discussion begins by focusing on the Talmud's interpretation (I A) of the Mishnah's two cases. He correctly regards the Talmud's reading of the Mishnah as implausible, for the Mishnah itself gives no indication that the number of witnesses is at issue. The Talmud's reading of the two cases simply has no foundation in the Mishnah's language. This forced interpretation is striking to Halivni and motivates him to investigate the source of this reading. He first turns to other interpretations of the Mishnah found in this section of the Talmud. Halivni considers the possibility that a statement attributed to Rab at b. Yeb. 88a is the basis of the puzzling interpretation cited above. Rab's statement, which seems to parallel the Talmud's interpretation of M. Yeb. 10:1, refers directly to that pericope.

> Said Rab, "They taught [that the woman must leave both her first and her second husband] only with reference to a case in which she married [the second husband] on the basis of a single witness [who testified that her first husband was dead]. But if she married [the second husband] on the basis of two witnesses' [testimony], she need not leave [him]."

Halivni compares Rab's reading of the Mishnah with the interpretation presented by the Talmud at b. Yeb. 87b. Rab explicitly states that the woman leaves her second husband only if she had remarried on the testimony of a single witness. Halivni claims, quite correctly, that this reading of the Mishnah's first case is in agreement with the Talmud's interpretation cited above. Yet, when we turn to the second case in the Mishnah (at S), Halivni notes, it becomes apparent that Rab's statement diverges from the Talmud's interpretation. In this case, we recall, the Talmud claims that a woman who remarries on the testimony of two witnesses may go back to her first husband when he returns. Rab, on the other hand, holds that under the same circumstances, she remains with her second husband. Rab's statement at b. Yeb. 88a cannot be the basis for the Talmud's interpretation of the Mishnah's second case, for the two statements are not in full agreement.

Having rejected the possibility that Rab's ruling is the basis of b. Yeb. 87b (I A), Halivni next considers an alternative interpretation of the Mishnah. Hanoch Albeck, a modern exegete of the Mishnah, proposes a quite different reading of M. Yeb. 10:1.[6] In Albeck's view, the distinction between the Mishnah's two cases has nothing to do with the number of witnesses who testify that the first husband has died. Rather, the decisive factor is whether or not the woman remarried with the permission of a court.

> Case 1: Woman remarried *with* permission of a court. When first husband returns, she must leave both men.
> Case 2: Woman remarried *without* permission of a court. When first husband returns, she goes back to him.

On Albeck's reading, the issue addressed by the pericope is the status of the woman's second marriage. In the Mishnah's first case, this marriage is deemed valid, for it has the court's approval. When the first husband reappears, therefore, the woman is fully married to two men and must leave both. In the second case, however, the woman has remarried without permission of a court, with the result that this marriage is null. She thus may return to her first husband.

In support of this interpretation, Albeck cites a parallel ruling, attributed to Simeon at T. Yeb. 11:4. Here again the court's approval is the single determinative factor. Simeon rules that if a court approves a woman's second marriage, and later the first husband returns, her sexual relationship with the second man is regarded as an intentional transgression. She must leave both men. If a woman remarries on her own initiative, however, she has committed only an unintentional transgression and may return to her first husband.

Albeck's interpretation of M. Yeb. 10:1 clearly is more plausible than the Talmud's. Albeck correctly recognizes that the number of witnesses who testify that the first husband has died in no way is pertinent to Mishnah's rules. In addition, unlike the Talmud's reading, Albeck's view is supported by a parallel source, T. Yeb. 11:4. It would appear, then, that Albeck's interpretation of M. Yeb. 10:1 offers the simplest reading of the pericope.

Halivni, however, believes that Albeck's interpretation suffers from two deficiencies. First, Albeck assumes that the phrase "without permission" (M. Yeb. 10:1S) means "without permission of a court." Yet, as Halivni notes, the word "court" does not appear in either of the Mishnah's cases. If the approval of the court is the decisive factor, it is odd, in Halivni's view, that the Mishnah makes no explicit reference to it. In this regard, he points to M. Tohorot 8:5, where the phrase "without permission" occurs but clearly makes no reference to a court. Second, Albeck's

---

[6] Hanoch Albeck, *Ššh Sdry Mšnh* (Jerusalem and Tel Aviv: Dvir, 1957) p. 47 and notes on p. 339.

interpretation fails to differentiate the phrase, "without permission," from the phrase, "without the consent of a court," which appears at the beginning of M. Yeb. 10:2. Since Albeck interprets the phrase "without permission" at M. Yeb. 10:1 to refer to a court, he must assume that the two quite distinct phrases used in successive pericopae have a single meaning. Although Halivni concedes that this is not impossible, he points out that Albeck offers no evidence to support this assumption. In all, Halivni finds Albeck's reading of the Mishnah unacceptable, for it is unsupported by the language of the pericope.

Halivni proceeds to present his own interpretation of M. Yeb. 10:1. The distinction between the two cases, in his view, is whether or not the woman remarried on the testimony of witnesses. The permission of a court plays no role here.

> Case 1: Woman remarries on the testimony of witnesses. When the first husband returns, she must leave both men.
> Case 2: Woman remarried on her own initiative, not on the testimony of any witnesses. When the first husband reappears, she must return to him.[7]

Halivni argues that this interpretation is preferable to Albeck's for it resolves the difficulties in Albeck's reading of the phrase "without permission." There is no need, Halivni claims, to introduce the question of the court's permission in order to make sense of the Mishnah's two contrasting cases. Moreover, the rules of M. Yeb. 10:2 refer explicitly to a court and so support Halivni's interpretation. M. Yeb. 10:2 rules that:

> A. If she remarried at the instruction of a court,
> B. she is to go forth,
> C. but she is exempt from [the requirement of bringing] an offering [required of those who unintentionally commit a transgression].
> D. If she did not remarry at the instruction of a court, she goes forth,
> E. and she is liable to [the requirement of bringing] an offering.

This pericope supplements M. Yeb. 10:1, on which it is dependent for its context and meaning. At issue here is whether the woman referred to at M. Yeb. 10:1 remarried with the permission of a court. The fact that this pericope refers explicitly to a court is strong evidence that at M. Yeb. 10:1 the approval of a court is not at issue. The language of M. Yeb. 10:2, then, lends credibility to Halivni's interpretation of M. Yeb. 10:1.

Finally, Halivni offers further textual support for his interpretation.

---

[7] Halivni immediately notes that, on his reading, the issue of the pericope is the status of the woman's second marriage, just as Albeck suggested. That is to say, in the first case, the woman is validly married to both husbands, while in the second case, her remarriage is null. *Meqorot Umesorot*, p. 100.

He cites the rule of b. Yeb. 11:5, which reads, in part, as follows:

A. A woman who went overseas with her husband,
B. and who came and reported, "My husband has died,"
C. [and] remarried on her own initiative
D. and again she went overseas and came and said, "My husband has died,"
E. [and] remarried on her own initiative
F. and again she went overseas and came and said, "My husband has died,"
G. and remarried on her own initiative,
H. and lo, all of them in fact are coming back—
I. she goes forth from all of them.
J. But she is permitted to remain married to the first.

Here a woman remarries on her own initiative, without either the testimony of other witnesses or the permission of a court. The result is that she may return to her first husband in the event that he reappears. This rule, then, is entirely consistent with M. Yeb. 10:1S, as Halivni reads it.

Having summarized Halivni's remarks, let us evaluate the merits of his exegetical program. Halivni's exegetical task, as illustrated by his comments to M. Yeb. 10:1, is carefully and narrowly defined. By focusing on forced interpretations in the Talmud, he permits the text itself to generate his questions. Thus, in the pericope we examined, Halivni chooses to comment only upon the Talmud's interpretation of Mishnah and ignores the Talmud's subsequent discussion of the principle that a single witness is trustworthy. Where the text poses no problems, Halivni offers no solutions. Moreover, having isolated a passage that requires his attention as an exegete, Halivni looks within rabbinic literature itself for the solution to his problem. As we noted, Halivni first examines other passages in the Talmud in order to find the basis of the interpretation which he regards as problematic. When this proves unsuccessful, Halivni turns his attention to the text under consideration, in this case, M. Yeb. 10:1. Here Halivni shows himself to be a skillful exegete of rabbinic literature. His sensitivity to the language of the text enables him to discover a straightforward and internally consistent reading of M. Yeb. 10:1's two cases. In all, Halivni takes the text seriously. He does not approach the Talmud with a thesis and then set out to find passages that will prove it. Rather, he allows the text to guide his exegesis, both in the questions which he poses and in the solutions which he offers.

Yet, when we turn from the results of Halivni's exegesis to the presuppositions of his method, several unresolved problems emerge. Halivni's exegetical program is generated by his fundamental assumption that the corpus of rabbinic literature can be divided into "sources" and "traditions." He further assumes that it is possible to recover the "sources" that stand behind certain confused "traditions." But these assumptions require a rigorous defense, which Halivni does not offer. Halivni must systematically address certain questions about the history of rabbinic literature in order to provide his exegesis with a firm foundation. What, for example, is Halivni's view of the formulation, transmission, and redaction of materials that have been preserved in the Talmud? In particular, Halivni should provide some criteria by which he can claim to determine that some texts have been preserved in their original form, while others have been transformed during the process of transmission into "traditions." Thus, although Halivni's exegetical comments to particular passages are insightful, his views about the historical and literary character of the Talmud as a whole have yet to be formulated in a clear, convincing manner.

Having completed this summary and analysis of Halivni's work, we are in a position to compare it with that of Shamma Friedman. The contrast between these two Talmudic scholars could not be more striking. Halivni is first and foremost an exegete of Talmud and approaches the text accordingly. The primary goal of his exegesis is to elucidate difficult passages in the text by locating the sources that explain the presence of forced interpretations. Friedman, as we recall, has other interests entirely. He is a theorist who develops and tests hypotheses about the formulation of the Talmudic text and hopes that, in the process, certain exegetical insights may emerge. His goals are to break apart the text into strata of named and anonymous materials, to account for the redactor's arrangement of these materials, and so to reconstruct the history of the text. It follows that the methods employed by each cannot be the same. For Halivni, parallel readings and textual variants are the tools of exegesis. Friedman, on the other hand, brings to the text an elaborate complex of theories and theses, which he then employs to analyze the text into its component parts. Finally, Halivni and Friedman differ in the scope of their work. Halivni comments only upon selected passages, for he allows the text to determine his questions. Friedman's remarks, by contrast, are meant to be a comprehensive analysis of an entire chapter of Talmud. This is required, he thinks, in order to test the theory that motivates his work. In short, Halivni and Friedman approach a single passage of Talmud with widely different assumptions about the task of exegesis. These assumptions determine both the questions each regards as critical and the methods each deems appropriate.

IV. ABRAHAM WEISS AS EXEGETE AND TEXT CRITIC
The Case of b. Berakot 35a

Roger Brooks
Brown University
and

Joseph M. Davis
Jewish Theological Seminary of America

ABSTRACT

The exegesis of the late Abraham Weiss, Yeshiva University, is grounded in his perception of logical gaps and inconsistencies in the text of the Talmud. Weiss thus allows the text itself to generate its own exegetical problems, and he uses other rabbinic materials and manuscript evidence to help solve them.[1]

Abraham Weiss spent the bulk of his scholarly career as Professor of Talmud at Yeshiva University,[2] where he wrote numerous articles and books on the development of the Talmud.[3] Weiss's material is marked by great attention to the Talmud's internal evidence of its formation. For the most part, he is not interested in the mere validation of *a priori* theories.[4] This paper provides one example of Weiss's exegesis, that of the opening unit of b. Berakot, Chapter Six. In order to place Weiss's comments in context, we shall first translate and outline the entire pericope. With the text firmly in hand, we shall summarize Weiss's comments, and provide a brief critique.

[1] Mr. Davis prepared the translation and outline of the relevant texts, b. Berakot 35a. The analysis of Weiss's comments was written by Mr. Brooks.
[2] For full information on Weiss's career, see "Prof. Abraham Weiss—A Biographical Sketch," *The A. Weiss Jubilee Volume, English section*, pp. 1-5.
[3] See Benjamin Weiss, "Rabbi A.-Weiss's Bibliography," ibid., Hebrew section, pp. 5-11.
[4] See Shammai Kanter, in J. Neusner, ed., *The Formation of Babylonian Talmud*, (Leiden:1970), pp. 87-88. Also, see Charles Primus, in J. Neusner, *The Modern Study of the Mishnah* (Leiden:1973), p. 197.

1. Translation
Joseph M. Davis

Mishnah Berakot 6:1

    A. What blessings does one say over fruit?
       Over fruit of the tree one says, "[Blessed art Thou, O Lord our God, King of the Universe], Who created the fruit of the tree,"
    C. except wine, over which one says, " . . . Who created the fruit of the vine."
    D. Over that which grows from the ground one says, " . . . Who created the fruit of the ground,"
    E. except bread, over which one says, " . . . Who brings forth bread from the earth."

Babylonian Talmud: Berakot 35a

    A. [The *gemara* begins with a question that forms the basis of the entire pericope.] From what [Scriptural verse can we derive] the law [that one is required to say a blessing before eating]?

    B. [A tannaitic saying derives the law that one must say blessings both before and after eating from Lev 19:24:] We have learned: [It is written concerning produce of the fourth year of a plant's growth, "All its fruit shall be] holy [worthy of] praisegiving unto the Lord."

    C. This teaches that one is required to say a blessing before and after eating [that fourth year produce]. [The saying interprets "praisegiving" as specifically referring to blessings. Since the Hebrew word for "praisegiving" [*hlwlym*] is plural, it means two blessings: one before eating, and one after.]

    D. [R. Aqiba now generalizes the conclusion.] On this basis, R. Aqiba said, "A man is forbidden to taste anything at all before he has said a blessing over it." [We thus have concluded that the law of blessings over food is derived from the word "praisegiving" in Lev 19:24.]

    E. [The *gemara* now objects to this conclusion. The law that one must say blessings over food cannot be based on the word "praisegiving," because, as we shall see at F–H, there are other laws that must be derived from that word. The *gemara* assumes that only one law can be derived from any word in Scripture (two laws from a word in its plural form). Another law derived from "praisegiving" therefore would leave no room for the interpretation offered above, at B.] And do these words, "holy, [worthy of] prasegiving [to the Lord] (*qdš hlwlym*)" mean [to teach that one must say blessings over food]? [Surely] they are required [as the basis for two other interpretations, now presented at F-H.]

F. [The two interpretations are based on the similarity between two words *hll*, to praise, and *hll*, to redeem or desanctify. Food that is in certain minor states of holiness—and in particular fourth year produce—may be redeemed by its owner for its value in cash. The money takes on the sacred character of the food, and the food becomes desanctified and may be eaten forthwith. The first interpretation is as follows:] [In using the word "praisegiving" (*hlwlym*) it is as if] the Merciful One said, "Redeem it [i.e. fourth year produce] ('*hlyh*) and then eat it ('*klyh*)." [The pay on '*hlyh* and '*klyh* is irrelevant to this interpretation.]

G. [We now present a second interpretation. It seeks to use the word "praisegiving" to show that the laws of the fourth year produce apply only to wine. Only wine had songs of praise (*hll*) sung over it when it was offered on the altar of the Temple in Jerusalem, cf. H. Only wine, therefore, requires redemption (*hll*) from the status of fourth year produce, or is subject to the laws of fourth year produce at all:] That which requires a song [of praise—wine—] requires redemption (*hlwl*) [and is thus subject to the laws of fourth year produce]. That which does not require a song [of praise—everything except wine—] does not require redemption [and is exempt from the laws of fourth year produce].

H. [We now provide Scriptural evidence that only wine required a song of praise when it was offered on the altar.] And it is as R. Samuel b. Nahmani taught in the name of R. Jonathan. For R. Samuel b. Nahmani taught in the name of R. Jonathan, "From what [Scriptural verse can we learn] that they sang songs [of praise at the altar] only over [offerings of] wine? As it is written [in Judg 9:13], 'And the vine said to them, "Shall I leave my wine, which makes God and men joyful?"' Granted that wine makes men joyful. But how does it make God joyful? [It must be through the songs of praise that were sung over the wine-offerings at the altar.] It follows from this that they sang songs of praise at the altar only over the wine-offerings."

I. [B-H therefore bring us to the following point. We have three interpretations, each of which bases a different law on the word "praisegiving" in Lev 19:24. The first (B-D) derives the law that one must say blessings before and after eating. The second (F) derives the law that fourth year produce may be redeemed and eaten. The third (G-H) derives the restriction that only wine is subject to the law of fourth year produce. But the existence of these three distinct interpretations posed a problem, as we saw earlier, at E. It is assumed that no more than a single law may be based on a single word in Scripture. To accept one of the interpretations, therefore, is to reject the other two, and leaves those laws, then, without a basis in Scripture. The *gemara* now sets out to solve this problem as best it can.] If one takes the position that all crops [and not just wine] are subject to the law of fourth year produce, then there is no problem. [Because then one will not need the interpretation of "praisegiving" that restricted the law of fourth year produce to wine. The other two interpretations both may be based on this word, because it is plural. On one "praisegiving" we base the first law; on the other "praisegiving" the second.]

J. [But this is only a partial solution. We object:] But for the one who takes the position that only wine is subject to the laws of fourth year produce, what is there to say? [He has a problem, because he requires all three interpretations of "praisegiving." While two laws may be derived from "praisegiving" (cf. I) three may not.]

K. [K does not advance the discussion but merely supplies a dispute between tannaim concerning whether the law of fourth year produce applies to all crops or only to wine.] As we have learned: R. Hiyya and R. Simeon b. Rabbi—one held the position that only wine is subject to the law of fourth year produce, and the other held the position that all crops are subject to the law of fourth year produce.

L. [The *gemara* now presents a solution to the problem posed at J.] There is no problem for the one who takes the position that only wine is subject to the law of fourth year produce, if he bases his view on a *gezerah shavah*. [A *gezerah shavah* is a particular mode of interpretation of Scripture. The connotations of a word as it is used in one context in Scripture are transferred to the same word used in a different context elsewhere in Scripture. If one bases on a *gezerah shavah* the position that only wine is subject to the law of fourth year produce, then one will not need to base that position on the word "praisegiving." Thus he will no longer be deriving too many laws from that word.]

M. [We now present the *gezerah shavah* on which we can base the law that only wine is subject to the law of fourth year produce.] As we have learned: Rabbi said, "It is written [in connection with the law of fourth year produce, Lev 19:25] 'to increase for you its produce (*tbw'tw*)'; and it is written elsewhere [Deut 22:9], 'and the produce (*wtbw't*) of the vineyard.' Just as in the latter verse [the word 'produce' specifically means the produce of a] vineyard, so too in the former verse [the word 'produce' must mean only the produce of a] vineyard." [Thus, by use of a *gezerah shavah*, we have derived the restriction that the only produce subject to the law of the fourth year of growth is the produce of a vineyard, namely wine.]

N. Therefore there is one "praisegiving" left [from which to derive the law that one must say] blessings [before and after eating.] [There are, as we said, two "praisegivings" available to be interpreted. If we use the *gezerah shavah* as the basis of the restriction to wine of the law of fourth year produce, then there is one "praisegiving" left over, which can be used as the basis of the requirement to say blessings over food.]

O. But if one does not accept the *gezerah shavah*, then from what [Scriptural verse can one derive the law that one must say] blessings [over food]? [Without the *gezerah shavah*, one is forced back into basing too many laws on the word "praisegiving." No answer is given to this objection. The *gemara* moves on to another objection.]

P. And even if one does accept the *gezerah shavah*, then [still only the requirement to say a blessing] after [eating] can be derived [from Scripture.] From what [Scriptural verse can one derive the requirement to say a blessing] before [eating]? [At I and again at N, we had based on a single "praisegiving" the law that one must say blessings over food. The *gemara* now objects: from a single "praisegiving" one cannot derive two blessings. Only one blessing can be derived; that is assumed to be the blessing after eating.]

Q. [An answer is given to the question just proposed.] This is no problem. [Although only the blessing after eating can be derived directly from Scripture, the requirement of saying a blessing before eating] can be derived by a *qal vehomer*. [A *qal vehomer* is a deduction from a weaker to a stronger case, *a minori a majus*.]

R. If one says a blessing [after eating], when he is full, then how much more so should he say a blessing [before eating] when he is still hungry? [If one acknowledges God when one's needs are satisfied, then how much more should one acknowledge Him when one is still in need of His aid.]

S. [But we now raise another objection. From Lev 19:24] we may derive [only the law that one must say blessings before and after drinking] wine. [For if we accept the *gezerah shavah* at L, then we must interpret the whole verse as referring only to wine, and the law of blessings, which we derived from the verse, as likewise referring only to wine.] From what [Scriptural source can we derive the requirement to say blessings before and after eating] other kinds [of food, except wine]?

T. [We attempt to answer the question by comparing wine to all other food.] We derive [the law that all food requires blessings] from [the fact that] wine [does]. Just as wine is something that is enjoyed, and requires blessings, so too everything that is enjoyed [that is, all food] requires blessings.

U. [This answer, however, proves too much. By this logic, wine and all other food would be subject to the same laws in all cases. But we know this is not true. So we object: Surely] we can make a distinction [between wine and other food]. Wine [—*kerem*, literally a vineyard—] is distinguished in that it is subject to the law of defective clusters [(cf. Deut 24:21), but other food is not. Perhaps only that which is subject to the law of defective clusters—i.e. wine—is subject to the law of blessings.]

V. [We answer:] [The case of] standing grain will prove [that the law of blessings is not restricted only to things subject to the law of defective clusters. For standing grain is not subject to the law of defective clusters, but we know that one is required to say a blessing after eating it, since Deut 8:9–10 states, "You shall eat bread without scarceness . . . and you will eat and be satisfied and bless the Lord your God."]

W. [But we now object: How can standing grain be compared to all other food?] Standing grain is distinguished [from other food] in that it is subject to the law of dough-offering [(cf. Num 15:21) but other food is not]. [Perhaps only that which is subject to the law of dough-offerings is subject to the law of blessings.]

X. [And we answer:] Wine proves [that this is not so. Wine requires blessings, but is not subject to the law of dough-offerings.]

Y. And so the argument turns full circle. The characteristics [of wine] are not like the characteristics [of standing grain] and the characteristics [of standing grain] are not like the characteristics [of wine].

Z. What [wine and bread] have in common is that both are things that are enjoyed and require blessings. Therefore, everything that is enjoyed must require blessings. [Thus, while we could not generalize from the case of either wine or bread individually to the case of all kinds of food, we now suggest that perhaps we can make that generalization from the case of wine and bread in combination.]

AA. [But we object: wine and bread, even in combination, can be distinguished from other kinds of food.] That which [wine and bread] have in common is that they were offered on the altar [in the Temple.] [Perhaps it is only those kinds of foods that could be offered on the altar that require blessing.]

BB. [BB–DD move away from the main stream of argument to discuss the question of how we may derive from Scripture the requirement to say blessings over olive oil. We work within the supposition just proposed at AA, that those kinds of foods that could be offered on the altar require blessings. So we begin by suggesting:] Therefore, olive oil [would require a blessing] because it was offered on the altar.

CC. [But we object:] Do we have to derive [the law that] olive oil [requires blessings] from the fact that it was offered on the altar? Does not [Scripture explicitly] call [both olive orchards and vineyards] *kerem*? [And therefore can we not make a direct inference that just as the produce of vineyards requires blessings, so too does the produce of olive orchards?] As it is written [Judg 15:5] "And it burnt both the shocks and the standing grain, together with the olive orchards (*kerem zayit*)."

DD. Answered R. Papa, "[Olive orchards] may be called *kerem zayit, but they are never called simply kerem.*" [Therefore olives are not governed by laws applying to *kerem*, a vineyard. We must derive the requirement to say blessings over olive oil from the fact that it was offered on the altar.]

EE. [The *gemara* now returns to the main stream of the argument, restating the question posed earlier at AA.] In any case, we still have a problem. [Wine and bread, and even olive oil] have in common that they were offered on the altar. [But how do we know that one is required to say a blessing over those kinds of foods not offered on the altar?]

FF. [We propose an answer.] Rather, we derive [the law that one is required to say blessings over all kinds of food] from [the requirement of saying blessings over] the "seven kinds." [The "seven kinds" are the seven foods mentioned at Deut 8:8, wheat, barley, wine, figs, pomegranates, olive oil, and date honey. At V, we interpreted Deut 8:10, "And you will eat and be satisfied and bless the Lord your God," as referring only to the bread mentioned in Deut 8:9. We now interpret it as referring to all seven kinds mentioned in 8:8.] Just as the "seven kinds" are things that are enjoyed and require blessings, so too everything that is enjoyed, [all food], should require blessings.

GG. [But as at T, we have now proved too much. By the same logic, the "seven kinds" and all other food would be subject to the same laws in all cases. We object:] The "seven kinds" are distinguished in that they are subject to the law of firstfruits. [Other food is not. Perhaps only food subject to the law of firstfruits is subject to the law of blessings. There is no answer, and we move on to another objection.]

HH. Furthermore, granted that [we may derive the requirement of saying a blessing] after [eating, from the explicit verse Deut 8:10], from what [Scriptural verse can one derive the requirement to say a blessing] before [eating? Deut 8:10 speaks only of saying a blessing after eating.]

II. [We asked a very similar question at P. We give the answer that we gave at Q.] The requirement of saying a blessing before eating is derived from a *qal vehomer*: if one says a blessing [after eating] when he is full, then how much more so should he say a blessing [before eating] when he is still hungry?

JJ. [We now back up the unanswered objection at GG with a further objection. At I, we said that there is no problem for the one who holds that all planted crops, and not just wine, are subject to the law of fourth year produce. We now raise an objection to that.] And for the one who takes the position that all planted crops are subject to the law of fourth year produce, there is no problem in saying that planted crops require blessings. But whence does he derive the law that one is required to say blessings over food that is not planted, for example meat or eggs or fish? [As at S, if the requirement to say blessings over food is based on "praisegiving" then it can govern only those kinds of foods spoken of at Lev 19:24, namely planted crops—those kinds of food subject to the law of fourth year produce.]

KK. We answer the objections at GG and JJ together.] Rather, [the extension to all food of the requirement of saying blessings is based on] a reasonable supposition: that a person is forbidden to derive any benefit from this world without saying a blessing.

2. Outline
Joseph M. Davis

I. A. 1. Question: What is the Scriptural basis for the law that one must say a blessing before eating?

2. Answer: The law is based on the word *hlwlym* in Lev 19:24. *Hlwlym*, praisegiving, is used in that verse as an epithet of fourth year produce. It is interpreted as meaning requiring blessings.

B. Objection to the answer of A.2. The word *hlwlym* cannot be used as a basis for the law that one must say a blessing before eating, because it is needed as the basis for two other laws, namely:

1. The law that fourth year produce may be redeemed.
2. The law that only wine is subject to the restrictions of fourth year produce.

C. Two solutions to the objection of B, and one rejected potential solution to that objection.
   1. First solution: We may reject the law that only wine is subject to the restrictions of fourth year produce, and take the contrary position. We will then have only two laws, one of which is the law of saying a blessing before eating, to be based on *hlwlym*. Since *hlwlym* is plural, it may be used as the basis for both laws.
   2. Second solution: Or we may accept that only wine is subject to the laws of fourth year produce, but base that law not on *hlwlym*, but on the word *tbw'tw* in the same verse. Once again, we will have only two laws based on *hlwlym*; one of them is the law that one must say a blessing before eating.
   3. Rejected potential solution: But we cannot both accept the law that only wine is subject to the restrictions of fourth year produce, and also base that law on *hlwlym*, because then we would be deriving too many laws from *hlwlym*.
D. Two objections to the second solution (C.2).
   1. The first objection is answered quickly.
      (a) Objection: One can derive from *hlwlym* only the law that one must say a blessing after eating, not before eating.
      (b) The requirement of saying a blessing before eating may be deduced logically. If one says a blessing after eating, when he is full, will he not say a blessing when he is still hungry?
   2. The second objection provokes a long series of rebuttals and further objections. There are six objections in the series, five of which are answered by rebuttals. The fifth, or next to the last, is not answered until the end of the pericope (F). After the fourth objection in the series, there is a discursus and the objection has to be repeated.
      (a) 1. Objection: One can derive from *hlwlym* only the law that one must say blessings over wine, not over other food.
         2. Rebuttal: Wine is like all other food in that both wine and other food give pleasure. If wine requires blessings, then all food must require blessings.
      (b) 1. Objection: But wine is unlike all other food in that it is subject to the law of defective clusters, but other food is not. Perhaps only that which is subject to the law of defective clusters is subject to the law of blessings.
         2. Rebuttal: That cannot be, because bread, which is not subject to the law of defective clusters, requires blessings (cf. Deut 8:9–10).

(c) 1. Objection: But not all food is like bread. Perhaps only food that is subject to the law of dough-offerings is subject to the law of blessings.
   2. Rebuttal: That cannot be, because wine is not subject to the law of dough-offerings, and it requires blessings.
(d) 1. Objection: Wine and bread have in common that they were offered on the altar. But not all kinds of food were offered on the altar. Perhaps only those kinds of food that were offered on the altar require blessings.
   2. Discursus: How should the requirement of saying blessings over olive oil be derived from Scripture?
      (a) It can be derived from the fact that olive oil was offered on the altar.
      (b) Objection to (a): There is a better way to derive the requirement. *Kerem* means both vineyard and olive orchard; therefore, the law of blessings, which applies to the produce of a *kerem*, should apply equally to olive oil as to wine.
      (c) Rebuttal to (b): *Kerem* means vineyard; *kerem zayit* means olive orchard.
   3. The objection at 1 is repeated: Perhaps only those kinds of food that were offered on the altar require blessings.
   4. Rebuttal: The seven kinds of food mentioned in Deut 8:8–10 all require blessings, but not all of them were offered on the altar.
(e) Objection: Perhaps only food that is subject to the law of firstfruits requires blessing. Wine and bread and olive oil and the seven kinds of food in Deut 8:8–10 are all subject to the law of firstfruits, but not all food is.
(f) 1. Objection: The commandment in Deut 8:8–10 only speaks of saying a blessing after eating. How can we derive the requirement of saying a blessing before eating?
   2. Rebuttal: The requirement of saying a blessing before eating may be deduced logically. If one says a blessing after eating, when he is full, will he not say a blessing before eating, when he is still hungry?

E. We now raise an objection to the first solution of the original problem (C.1).
Objection: Even if one takes the position that all planted crops are subject to the law of fourth year produce, then still one may derive from *hlwlym* only the requirement to say blessings over planted crops. How can one derive the requirement of saying

blessings over food that is not planted, such as meat, eggs, or fish?

F. We answer simultaneously the objection just posed at (E), and the still unanswered objection of (D.2.e).
Answer: The extension to all food of the requirement to say blessings before and after eating is based on a reasonable supposition. It is reasonable to suppose that a person is forbidden to derive benefit from this world without saying a blessing.

3. Summary and Critique
Roger Brooks

My analysis of Abraham Weiss's[5] comments is in two parts, a summary and a brief critique. As we shall see, Weiss provides his readers with questions based on inconsistencies within the text. He then resolves these textual difficulties by adducing the evidence of variant texts and manuscripts. His goal, then, is to establish a reliable version of the passage, not through harmonization or contradictions, but on the basis of solid textual evidence. With this new version in hand, Weiss gives us an account of the text's history, explaining how the present, in his view, corrupt, edition came into being. His program thus is well-rounded and full, comprising questions, answers, and explanations.

Weiss begins his analysis by reviewing the passage's main question: What is the Scriptural basis for the requirement of saying a blessing before and after eating? According to Weiss, the simplest solution to this question is provided by Lev 19:24, which states: "All fruit shall be holy, [worthy of] praisegiving (*hlwlym*) to the Lord" (cf. B). Because the word "praisegiving" appears in the plural form, the verse is suited to serve as the basis for two blessings, one before the meal and one after. The Talmud's ensuing discussion (C–O), we recall, rejects this straightforward solution. Rather it claims that one of the two "praisegivings" mentioned in Lev 19:24 is used to derive the restrictions applying to four-year-old vines (D–I). As explained above (cf. I), the plural "praisegivings" can serve as the basis for at most two laws. It therefore no longer is possible to derive from this single word blessings before and after the meal.

With this summary of the pericope's basic issues in hand, Weiss raises two logical questions, which we shall take up in turn. Weiss's first question concerns the statement at H, that Lev 19:24 justifies blessings before and after the meal, even if one of the "praisegivings" already has been used to derive the restrictions of fourth year produce. This lemma, Weiss claims, poses a problem, since a parallel case, M–O, gives rise to a

---

[5] Weiss's comments to this section are found in an untitled article that appeared in *Horeb*, Vol. 10:19–20, pp. 1–6.

quite different response. At M–O, we recall, one of Lev 19:24's two "praisegivings" has been used as the scriptural basis for the restrictions of a four-year-old wine. As a result, only one "praisegiving" remains from which to derive the two blessings, before and after eating. This, of course, is precisely the same shortage of scriptural prooftexts as at H. Within the logic of the Talmud, Lev 19:24 ought to be adequate justification for only one blessing, the one after the meal (so O). Thus the Talmud quite logically asks (O), "Whence does one derive the requirement to say a blessing *before* eating?" Why, Weiss wishes to know, does this same problem not arise at H, a lemma that presents precisely the same situation?

Weiss's second question arises because the Talmud overlooks an obvious solution to its basic problem. At issue, we recall, is how to find scriptural bases for two blessings, assuming that one of Lev 19:24's "praisegivings" already has been used to derive the restrictions of four-year-old vines. The answer, it seems to Weiss, should be found in Deut 8:10, which states, "You shall eat and be full, and then bless the Lord your God." Later in this very pericope (U), the verse provides an adequate basis for the requirement to bless after the meal. The single remaining "praisegiving" would justify the blessing before the meal. The question, then, is why the Talmud does not appeal to Deut 8:10 in order to solve its problem.

Before turning to Weiss's solutions, let us ask how Weiss frames his questions. Weiss's inquiries are entirely fitting to the nature and scope of his source, for they derive from his identification of logical gaps or inconsistencies in the text. Because of a contradiction between two stichs (H and M), Weiss isolates a problem requiring his attention as an exegete. That is to say, the text itself determines what questions are deemed important.

In the next step of his argument, Weiss disposes of those two problems in a single motion. He adduces a parallel version of the passage, contained in the Florence manuscript:

Printed Edition

N. If one does not accept the *gezerah shavah*, then from what [scriptural verse can the law that one must say] blessings [over food be derived]? [Without the *gezerah shavah*, we recall, one is forced to base more than two laws on the word "praisegiving" in Lev 19:24.]

Codex Florence

1. [Let us assume that we deal with a case in which] one does not use a *gezerah shavah*. [Again, the result is that no "praisegivings" remain from which to derive the rules of blessings.]

O. And even if one does accept the *gezerah shavah* [leaving a single "praisegiving" from which to derive the two blessings],

granted that [in this case] one must say] a blessing after [eating, because of Deut 8:10's injunction].	2. Granted that [in this case] one must say] a blessing after [eating, because of Deut 8:10's injunction].
From what [scriptural verse can one derive the requirement to say a blessing] before [eating]?	3. From what [scriptural verse can one derive the requirement to say a blessing] before [eating]?

The Florence manuscript differs from the standard printed version only at O. MS Florence lacks the first clause of O, and so refers only to a case in which neither of the two "praisegivings" mentioned in Lev 19:24 is available for the purpose of justifying blessings before or after the meal. One of the "praisegivings" is used as the basis for the restrictions of fourth year produce in general. The other is taken as indicating the specific injunction concerning four-year-old vines. According to Codex Florence, both "praisegivings" have been assigned to these other laws, and so Lev 19:24 has no relationship to the requirement to bless over food at all.

Weiss claims that this variant reading solves the pericope's two problems. As we recall, the first problem arises when we compare the statements at H and M–O. In both cases, according to the printed edition, a single "praisegiving" remains from which to derive two blessings. Nevertheless, one case (H) gives rise to "no difficulties," while the other (M–O) draws in its wake a lengthy explanation (P–Q). The Florence manuscript, for its part, posits a situation at M (unlike that of H) in which there are no "praisegivings" at all from which to derive the laws of blessings. The two cases actually refer to separate circumstances, and so the logical contradiction within the passage is eliminated.

Weiss's second question also is answered by reading the passage in line with the Florence manuscript. Deut 8:10, ignored by the printed version, now is taken as the prooftext for blessing after eating. The statement that we can derive from Scripture the requirement to bless after meals (2) must refer to Deut 8:10, for Lev 19:24 is completely unavailable as a prooftext.

With these problems and their solutions in hand, Weiss now proceeds to the next logical question, how did the printed version of the text come into being? That is to say, he provides us with an account of the text's history. Weiss posits that the Florence manuscript represents the original version of the text. At some point, a copyist added a marginal gloss, "And if one does accept the *gezerah shavah* . . . " (= first clause of O). This note was intended to set up the entire discussion following R, turning from a case in which Lev 19:24 is unavailable as a prooftext (N–Q) to a case in which one "praisegiving" remains (R–II). The note, then, should have been attached to the beginning of R. Instead, Weiss claims, the phrase was erroneously added before O, for both stichs (O and R) begin, "Granted that. . . ." Had the note been placed properly, the passage would read:

> O. [If one does not accept the *gezerah shavah*, so that no praise-givings remain], granted that [he must say a blessing] after [eating, because of Deut 8:10's injunction]. Whence [does one derive the requirement to say a blessing] before [eating] . . . ?

> R. And even if one does accept the *gezerah shavah*, granted that [the law of blessings applies to] wine. Whence [does one derive the requirement to bless] all other sorts of food?

Instead, of course, the phrase was misplaced, creating the present version of the text, with all its complications.

Let us now evaluate Weiss's approach. His questions prove him to be a sophisticated and insightful exegete. His lines of inquiry are determined solely from a straightforward reading of the text. Furthermore, Weiss's solutions to these problems are inductive. He answers textual questions on the basis of solid evidence, not of *a priori* assumptions. His use of MS Florence provides him with facts that resolve the text's problems. In short, his answers are not mere announcements that a line or section is out of place. Rather he presents carefully reasoned attempts to regain the logically consistent text that he believes underlies the sometimes corrupt printed edition. Finally, it is noteworthy that Weiss's analysis is comprehensive. He succinctly notes the text's problems, and then provides answers. This is followed by his account of how the text before us might have developed. His reader thus is not left with isolated remarks about this or that detail, but is led from the "original" version to the text before us. Weiss's well-rounded work is highly satisfying, for he asks precisely the question which all readers of the Talmud pose: How do we make sense of the text before us?

REDACTION AND FORMULATION
The Talmud of the Land of Israel and the Mishnah

Jacob Neusner
Brown University

ABSTRACT

Seeing rabbinic documents as whole and autonomous works allows for the differentiation of one document from another and for the study of each in its historical and social context. The description of any rabbinic document must begin with the identification of its regularities, its ubiquitous rules of formulation.

An examination of the gross literary and redactional traits of the Palestinian Talmud shows that its editors had a redactional program. The document exhibits a tendency to move from a close reading of the Mishnah and Tosefta to a more general inquiry into the principles of a Mishnah-passage, and finally to more general reflections on law(s) not self-evidently related to the Mishnah-passage. There is little evidence of concern to establish encompassing structural or syntactic patterns. These facts suggest that, unlike the Mishnah, the redaction of units of discourse in the Palestinian Talmud was distinct from, and took place later than, the formulation of those units. Already formulated materials were arranged according to a few general redactional rules.

i. *Seeing the Whole Whole*

Grasping whole and complete documents produced by the rabbis of late antiquity is not easy because of the sheer size of the texts. Perhaps that is why people limit their perspectives to exegesis of bits and pieces of the whole. They take as the exegetical task the comparison of one bit of one document with a slice of a different document. In doing so, they obliterate all lines of historical, hence also social, demarcation. For, failing to see any document whole and complete, they cannot take a sighting on its context in history and society, its distinguishing and characteristic traits of style and substance. Accordingly, sighting a document in its own time and place is never attempted. It follows that no one attempts to describe the distinctive viewpoint of a document as a whole and to ask about why the people behind the document chose to say what they do rather than something else, to express themselves in one way rather than another. Everything is read in one enveloping context, established by such circumlocutions as "the rabbis," or "Talmudic Judaism," or just "Judaism," or "the Midrash" or "the Talmud." Indeed, since medieval and even early modern writers and compilers followed established literary conventions and produced compilations of exegesis of Scripture (*midrashim*), it has now become possible to treat as a single, continuous, essentially non-historical and non-contextual corpus of midrashic materials, writings extending over nearly fifteen hundred years and three continents.

Seeing the whole in a whole way defines the first step in differentiation of one document from another. It allows us for the first time to ask about the viewpoint expressed by one group of compilers or redactors in making up or selecting and then putting things together as they did, as distinct from the viewpoint expressed by some other group in dealing with materials whether of a parallel or a different sort. Rather than assuming there is a single, "rabbinic" or "midrashic" viewpoint on anything and everything including aesthetics, we may then investigate the parts of Judaism of the rabbinic sort, prior to asking whether and how they fit together and why they have reached their present condition as a whole. In the absence of historical differentiation and description, literary criticism of rhetoric and other aesthetic conventions of expression seems unlikely to make much progress beyond the mere guess-work and free-association that now prevail. But the ancient and medieval rabbis did not make things up as they went along. They labored within constraints of convention and tradition, at the same time vastly expanding and enriching the inherited corpus through their own imagination and theological and rhetorical inventiveness. Contemporary literary criticism can do no less than deal with a document in its context of both continuity and creativity, rather than as an undifferentiated mess of proof-texts.

If we wish to see a document as a whole, the first thing we must look for is regularities, rules of formulation everywhere present. From such simple and external things, and only from them, we may then proceed to posit recurrent principles or ideas: the things the document's author(s) or compiler(s) wished to say. The former procedure is not subjective, the latter may be. In the former case we look for such things as recurrent particles or word-groupings, syntactic patterns, word-choices and how they work—facts of rhetoric and expression. These either are there, or they are not there. No one can tell us that he does not see them—or (as is common in theological and literary-critical fields) he does not "agree." If, by contrast, we start our work with an account of what we think the text wishes to tell us, the fundamental and generative problematic the document takes up, we may be right, but in the charged contemporary context of discourse, it may not matter very much. For everyone's opinion is as good as everyone else's, concerning a text no one has studied beginning to end anyhow. Once more the sheer volume of any significant document presents formidable obstacles to rational and informed discourse. If, as in the present case, one proposes to make judgments never before attempted, it is therefore best to begin at the beginning.

ii. *The Talmud of the Land of Israel*

The Talmud of the Land of Israel (also: the Palestinian Talmud, Yerushalmi, or the Jerusalem Talmud), ca. A.D. 400, consists of thirty-nine tractates, each one devoted to a corresponding tractate of the Mishnah, concluded in ca. A.D. 200. The Mishnah, for its part, is divided into sixty-two tractates (excluding reference to Abot) and stands behind not only the Palestinian Talmud but also the Babylonian one. The two Talmuds, then, took shape around a single prior document. Each takes up its own selection of Mishnah-tractates.

The first translation into English of the Talmud under discussion is accomplished. I have completed twenty-nine of the thirty-nine tractates, in twenty-four volumes, and others, mainly my students, are working on the other ten tractates, to appear in ten further volumes, thirty-four in all, under the title, *The Talmud of the Land of Israel. A Preliminary Translation and Explanation* (Chicago, 1982ff.: The University of Chicago Press). Volume 35 serves as an introduction.

It seems to me essential to translate into our own language any text subject to sustained and systematic study. First of all, we thereby make available for all to see precisely what is subject to discussion. Second, we make a commitment to the meaning of the text at every point, thereby exposing the numerous points at which matters really are not very clear. If the translation retains a close relationship to the original, as mine does, and constitutes more than a mere paraphrase (unlike that of Moise Schwab, *Le Talmud de Jérusalem. Traduit pour la première fois en français* [Paris, 1871-1890]), then the literary-critical labor will be shown to rest not on guess-work or subjective impressions. Nor will it depend on random selection of odd and interesting things. Rather it will take up the entire text, its gross and prevailing traits. If and when systematic historical and literary work on the Talmud of the Land of Israel gets under way in the State of Israel, colleagues there, for their part, will find they have to translate the entire document into Israeli Hebrew. The alternative is a text never subject to minute analysis, results never available for testing and replication.

The translation I have made is called preliminary, and I wish briefly to digress to explain why. The tentative character of the translation governs the status of all results based upon it.

My translation into English of the Talmud of the Land of Israel ("Palestinian Talmud," "Yerushalmi") is provisional, even though it is not apt to be replaced for some time. It is preliminary, first, because a firm and final text for translation is not in hand; second, because a modern commentary of a philological and *halakic* character is not yet available; and, third, because even the lower criticism of the text has yet to be undertaken. Consequently, the meanings imputed to the Hebrew and Aramaic words and the sense ascribed to them in this translation at best are merely a first step. When a systematic effort at the lower criticism of the extant text has been completed, a complete philological study and modern dictionary along comparative lines made available, and a commentary based on both accomplished, then the present work will fall away, having served for the interim. Unhappily, as I said, that interim is apt to be protracted. Text-critics, lexicographers, and exegetes are not apt to complete their work on Yerushalmi within this century or even the next.

The purpose of my preliminary translation is to make possible a set of historical and religious-historical studies on the formation of Judaism in the Land of Israel from the closure of the Mishnah to the completion of the Talmud of the Land of Israel and the time of the composition of the first midrashic compilations. Clearly, no historical, let along religious-historical, work can be contemplated without a theory of the principal document and source for the study, the Palestinian Talmud. No theory can be attempted, however tentative and provisional, without a complete, prior statement of what the document appears to wish to say and how its materials seem to have come to closure. It follows that the natural next steps, beyond my now-finished history of Mishnaic law and account of the Judaism revealed in that history, carry us to the present project. Even those steps, when they are taken, will have to be charted with all due regard to the pitfalls of a translation that is preliminary, based upon a text that as yet has not been subjected even to the clarifying exercises of lower criticism. Questions will have to be shaped appropriate to the parlous state of the evidence. No one can proceed without a systematic account of the evidence and a theory of how the evidence may, and may not, be utilized.

Let us now turn to the question with which we began: how to see the whole whole. It must be emphasized that the sole acceptable method is inductive inquiry. Everything that follows assumes we know nothing *a priori* about the Talmud under study. We must reason about its character without prior information of any kind, even concerning the presence of a completed document, the Mishnah, around which the (nascent) compilation of the Palestinian Talmud is arranged and shaped.

iii. *The Starting Point*

To describe the Talmud before us we first take up the whole and proceed to ask about its principal components or constituents.

Looking at the Talmud whole, we notice two totally distinct sorts of materials: statements of law, then discussions of and excursions on those statements. No substantial presuppositions to the text are demanded to justify our declaring these two sorts of materials to be, respectively, primary and constitutive, secondary and derivative. Calling the former the Mishnah-passage, the latter, the Talmud (proper), imposes no *a priori* judgment formed separate from the literary evidence in hand. We might as well call the two, "the code," and "the commentary." The result would be no different.

In fact, as we see everywhere, the Talmud is made up of two elements, each with its own literary traits and program of discussion. Since the Mishnah-passage at the head of each set of Talmudic units of discourse defines the limits and determines the theme and, generally, the problematic of the whole, our attention is drawn to the traits of the Mishnaic-passages as a group. As we shall see in a moment, here, of course, a certain measure of descriptive work is complete. (I refer to my *History of the Mishnaic Law of Purities* [Leiden, 1977]. XXI. *The Redaction and Formulation of the Order of Purities in Mishnah and Tosefta*. This is cited below.) But even if we for the first time saw these types of pericopae of the Talmud (embedded as they are in the Talmud and separated from one another), we should discern that they adhere to a separate and quite distinctive set of literary canons from what follows and surrounds them. Hence at the outset, with no appreciable attention to anything beyond the text, we should distinguish two "layers" of the Talmud and recognize that one such "layer" is formed in one way, the other in another way. (I use "layer" for convenience only; it is not a suitable metaphor.)

As I just said, if we were to join together the Mishnah-pericopae, we should notice that they are stylistically and formally coherent, and also different from everything else in the compilation before us. Accordingly, for stylistic reasons alone we are on firm ground in designating the "layer" before us as the base-point for all further inquiry. For the Mishnah-"layer" is uniform, while the Talmud-"layer" is not. Hence, the former, itself undifferentiated, provides the point of differentiation, and the latter, the diverse materials subject to differentiation. In the first stage in the work of making sense of the Talmud and describing it whole, the initial criterion through which the Talmud's diverse types of units of discourse—complete discussions, discontinuous with other such discussions fore and aft—will be this: the diverse relationships to the Mishnah's rule exhibited by the Talmud's several units of discourse. Let me now expand and qualify this point, for it is the principle of my opening initiative of taxonomy and typology.

To amplify what I have said: since the Palestinian Talmud carries forward and depends upon the Mishnah, to describe that Talmud whole, we have to begin with its relationship to the Mishnah, its own starting point. While the Mishnah admits to no antecedents and alludes to and cites nothing prior to its own materials, a passage of the Talmud may ordinarily be incomprehensible without knowledge of the passage of the Mishnah around which its materials center. Yet to describe and define the Talmud, we should grossly err if we were to say it is only, or mainly, a commentary on the Mishnah. We may not even say—though it is a step closer to the truth—that the Talmud before us is a commentary and secondary development of the Mishnah and important passages of the Tosefta.[1] Units of discourse that serve these sorts of materials stand side by side with many that do not. The Palestinian Talmud is essentially autonomous of the Mishnah. Accordingly, while describing the Talmud requires attention to the interplay between the Talmud and the Mishnah and Tosefta, the diverse relationships between the Talmud and one or the other of those two documents constitute only one point of description and differentiation. For the Talmud is in full command of its own program of thought and inquiry. True, it chose what, in the Mishnah, will be analyzed, and what is not. There could be no Talmud without the Mishnah and Tosefta. But knowing only those two works, we could never have predicted the character of the Talmud's discourse at any point.

Still, as I said, the Mishnah serves at the outset to permit us to gain perspective on the character of Yerushalmi. The Mishnah exhibits remarkable unities of literary and redactional traits. By that standard our Talmud presents none. Accordingly, while whatever materials reached the framers of the Mishnah have been revised by them in line with a single and simple literary and redactional program, the same is not apt to have been the case for the Talmud of the Land of Israel. Whatever the stages of redaction of the document as a whole, let alone its components, we may say with certainty that the people ultimately responsible for the document as we have it did not do to the materials in their hands what the framers of the Mishnah did to theirs. The contrary is the case. Units of discourse framed in some prior setting have been preserved as is (though we do not know to what extent as to detail). They were drawn together whole and complete with other such essentially fixed and final units of discourse. That is the principal result of what follows. The Mishnah is constructed out of a

---

[1] For the present purpose, we may define Tosefta simply as materials formulated in the language and syntax of the Mishnah, but not now included in the Mishnah as we know it. That definition is inductive, as an examination of any of Tosefta's materials cited below [= underline] will indicate.

severely limited repertoire of syntactic and rhetorical forms. The Talmud is diffuse and stylistically promiscuous. The former is tight, the latter loose; the former amply articulated syntactically, the latter remarkably elliptical; the former uniform and stylistically cogent, the latter not. The former speaks in whole sentences, the latter in shorthand and abbreviation, notes toward discourse never amply articulated. Accordingly, it suffices to state as fact, beyond doubt, that what the Mishnah's redactors did to the Mishnah, Yerushalmi's redactors did not do to Talmud Yerushalmi. Our first task is to attempt to describe what they did do. But before proceeding, let us review the principal traits of the composition of the Mishnah. That exercise permits us to gain perspective as we proceed to the work of describing those of the Talmud of the Land of Israel.

iv. *Redaction and Formulation: Contrast to the Mishnah*

Our first task is to ask about the formulation and redaction of the Talmud of the Land of Israel as we know it—the end product in our hands—and not the formation, in earlier times, of ideas or whole discussions now contained within the document. The nature of the antecedent materials can only be determined when we have described what must be deemed the work of ultimate redaction and decided that is the case whether or not the process also included systematic formulation, or reformulation, of units of discourse already completed.

When I undertook to ask about the role of redaction in the formulation of the Mishnah, working on the division of Purities as my sample (roughly 26% of the entire Mishnah), I began from the outside and worked my way inside. To review the process and its principal results, I began by asking this fundamental question: If all we had were a mass of words, how should we know where one thing stops and another starts? The first question is not difficult definitively to answer. We know that the mass of words is to be broken up for the Mishnah's division of Purities, into twelve principal divisions, tractates, uneven in length, because the subject of one long sequence of undifferentiated words ends, and a new subject begins. There are, accordingly, lines of demarcation obviously and clearly drawn by the shift in theme or primary topic of discussion. What is blocked out, moreover, is consistent in its devotion to that given theme or primary topic, rarely dealing with a subject wholly irrelevant to said theme. It follows that the principal mode of organization of masses of words is thematic, and, as is clear, the principal lines of division will be, first, into tractates devoted to their respective, diverse topics. What is important is that that fact is shown on the basis of the internal character of the document, not merely of the *post factum* way in which exegetes, copyists, and printers organized matters.

Having proved that the Mishnah is organized, in its principal divisions, in accord with the unfolding of thematic and logical principles, I proceed to ask about the delineation of intermediate divisions of the principal ones. I avoid the word, "chapters," because it can only yield confusion with the present chapters, which are the work of copyists and printers, perhaps even of the earliest exegetes. These tell us nothing whatsoever about the original intent of the people who come before, and stand behind, the document, but only about the exegetical perceptions of the people who come afterward. How on the basis of internal evidence are intermediate divisions to be discerned? Having shown that the redactors not only organize their materials topically but also lay out the discussion of that topic in accord with its logically sequential parts, I am on firm ground in maintaining that one criterion for a demarcation-line of undifferentiated columns of words of a Mishnah tractate, or principal division, will be a shift in topic or theme. What applies to, and emerges from, the whole surely must be asked to serve as criterion for what pertains also to the parts. There is, moreover, a second important criterion of delineation, and that is, recurrent grammatical patterns or arrangement of words. This entails inquiry into the large-scale interplay between theme and form, between what is said and how it is said.

The first thing we notice when we study a Mishnah tractate from its opening sentence is that, when the subject changes, the formulary pattern tends to shift too. A given subtopic of a topical unit—a principal division—will be expressed in a distinctive pattern of syntax. When discussion of that subtopic ends and treatment of what is clearly meant as a new subtopic begins, syntactical patterns change also. These syntactical patterns, moreover, turn out to be divisible into two broad categories, tight and loose. The former sort of syntactical pattern will govern the layout of words for each and every conception, thought, or rule devoted to a given subtopic. The latter sort of pattern will not, but, rather, will emerge chiefly at the commencement of the expression of each and every conceptual unit. The former is therefore called an internally-unitary formulary pattern, in that the formulary pattern everywhere governs the internal construction of what is expressed. The latter is named an externally-unitary formulary pattern, in that the formulary pattern is external to what is expressed and imposed primarily upon the opening clauses of a conceptual unit. The remainder of the unit then will proceed in unpatterned sentences or clauses. To put matters more descriptively, we are unable to discern, in sentences which follow the commencement of the matter, any systematic pattern at all.

These results impose the requirement of the further definition, differentiation, and analysis of the recurrent patterns by which sentences are constructed. The reason obviously is that, once we recognize intermediate divisions because of the congruence of form and theme, we come to the stage of the analysis of form. The appropriate framework for form-analysis is the redactionally sizable, intermediate unit. For it is within the setting of the intermediate division that the formalization of language becomes self-evident and uncontingent. It ceases to be a subjective observation that things seem to be stereotype, only when we see that, within circumscribed, but sizable sequences of sentences, things indeed are not random but recurrent. It is within that same framework that we discern precisely what patterning of language is undertaken, how thought is reduced not merely to words, but to words laid out in distinctive, recurrent syntactical structures.

It is at this point that we must define the smallest unit of formal analysis, which I call, for the Mishnah, "the cognitive unit." A cognitive unit is the formal and formalized result of a single cogent process of cognition, that is, analysis of a situation and statement of a rule pertaining to it, or some other, similar intellectual process. The Mishnah's smallest whole and irreducible literary-conceptual units are the end-result of a single sequence, or process, of thought. Formal or formulary traits of such a unit commonly occur at the outset or in the first element of the result of cognition to be set into words and given linguistically formal character. After that point in the unit, what follows usually exhibits no equivalent formalization. The remainder of the cognitive unit will generally consist of simple declarative sentences exhibiting no recurrent pattern and lacking all syntactical distinctiveness. The cognitive unit rarely stands by itself but is grouped together with other such units, devoted to a single principle or theme and exhibiting a single, distinctive syntactical trait or preference. Accordingly, the form-analytical work yields the result that the cognitive unit is shaped within the processes of organization of the intermediate (and principal) divisions of the division of Purities and the others as well. This means that the work of giving formalized verbal expression to cognitive units and the work of organizing them into groups go together and reciprocally govern one another's results.

To state the historical result simply: The Mishnah's formulation and its organization are the result of the work of a single generation of tradent-redactors, tradents, who formulate units of thought, and redactors, who organize aggregations of said units of thought. The Mishnah is not the product of tradents succeeded by redactors. It is not possible upon the basis of objective, internal literary evidence revealed by Mishnah itself to specify much that the formulation derives from the period before that of redaction itself.

We may rapidly relate these final results to the document at hand. In the case of the Palestinian Talmud, the principle of organization is provided by the Mishnah. Tractates begin and end where the Mishnah does. (There are some exceptions, in which we have no Talmud for a Mishnah-chapter.) Accordingly, if all we had were a mass of words, we should know the beginning and end of a tractate of our Talmud precisely as we do in the case of the Mishnah, because the point of demarcation is

identical. When it comes to the unfolding of intermediate divisions—
"units of discourse" in my earlier paragraphs—we are in a different
situation entirely. A glance at any volume of my translation will show
that, in nearly all cases, the Talmud's discourse attached to a given
pericope of the Mishnah runs through two or more completed units of
discourse. In general, therefore, the principle of organizing a discussion
is not supplied solely and completely by the logical or other exegetical
requirements of a passage of the Mishnah. The principle by which a
discussion is inaugurated, worked out, and concluded, is different from
that of the Mishnah in general and also from that supplied by a given
intermediate unit of the Mishnah in particular cases. The third stage in
the inquiry into the Mishnah therefore is not relevant. Since the intermediate divisions of the Yerushalmi are not demarcated by the requirements of the Mishnah, we cannot attempt to relate the delineation of
those units of formal traits pertinent to the Mishnah. As we know full
well, formal considerations do not come into play in the Talmud before
us in so rigid and disciplined a way as they do in the formulation of the
Mishnah's ideas. It must follow that the work of ultimate redaction of
the Palestinian Talmud is wholly separate from the work of formulation
of divisions of discourse. (Admittedly, revisions in details of the text can
have taken place at that ultimate or even penultimate stage of
organization and closure.)

The upshot is that the framers of the Talmud of the Land of Israel
refer constantly to the Mishnah, but do not see themselves as bound by
patterns of formulation and redaction, let alone its program and problems. They have in hand, or have created, diverse sorts of units of discourse, some of them essentially exegetical and tied to the Mishnah,
others doing the same for Tosefta, still others of a quite separate literary
character and substantive purpose. To describe the Talmud as a whole,
we have to develop a taxonomy of its several types of units of discourse.

v. *Yerushalmi's Redactional Program*

Developing a taxonomy of the units of discourse contained within
the Talmud of the Land of Israel, we seek to describe gross redactional
traits. The question then is simple: What kinds of units of discourse does
the document exhibit and how are they arranged? The answer to this
second question should yield a first glimpse at the redactional program
of the ultimate framers of the Talmud. Once we differentiate among the
materials in the hands of the arrangers of the whole, we also may
observe what principles, if any, guide their work.

For the present purpose, seeking the most general traits of the whole, a
modest probe suffices. I review five tractates, a small one (Niddah), a very
large one (Sanhedrin), an egregious one (Baba Meṣia), and two medium

ones (Nedarim and Sukkah). The egregious category is defined by Saul Lieberman's landmark study, "The Talmud of Caesarea" (*Supplement to Tarbiṣ* 2 [Jerusalem, 1931]), in which the tractates of the civil law, Baba Qamma, Baba Meṣia, and Baba Batra, are shown to be different from all others in the Talmud of the Land of Israel. There Lieberman maintains that these tractates were edited in Caesarea about 350 or so, that is, a half-century prior to the closure of the Yerushalmi as a whole. The point of interest is whether the rough procedures with which we begin replicate Lieberman's basic judgment as to the egregious character of these tractates. In fact they do.

By unit of discourse I mean simply a discussion on a single topic, beginning either at a pericope of the Mishnah or at the point at which said topic is raised, ending either at the next pericope of the Mishnah or at the point at which some other topic is introduced, respectively. What is important is the sequence of these units. Where there is direct analysis of the Mishnah, or, at the very least, inquiry into the Scriptural foundations of the Mishnah-pericope at hand, the unit of discourse presenting such analysis or inquiry normally is the opening one in a sequence. Among the 335 Mishnah-pericopes in the tractates named above, only 26 units of discourse pertinent to the Mishnah-rule at hand, less than 8% of the whole, do not inaugurate the sequence of units. (I exclude reference to the handful of Mishnah-pericopes in which there is no analysis of the Mishnah-law at all. I also omit reference to the passages in which Tosefta's complement to the Mishnah's rule stands at the commencement of the discussion. These tend to balance each other out.) Accordingly, it is clear that the usual redactional practice was to take a completed unit of discourse pertinent to the Mishnah and to place it at the commencement of discourse on the passage of the Mishnah at hand.

There is a further tendency to include in that opening unit, or in the one(s) immediately following, materials now found in Tosefta pertinent to the Mishnah. Accordingly, these Toseftan passages will be cited either to amplify and extend the Mishnah's rule or otherwise to facilitate discourse about (or around) it. In Baba Meṣia, that is normally the case. Since Lieberman is surely right, the Caesarean Talmud shows us what the Talmud of the Land of Israel looked like, at least in the estimation of some circles or schools, at the outset. In that case it consisted, in the main, of the Mishnah's rule followed by Tosefta's amplification, then some (rather desultory) discourse, more commonly on the latter than on the former. If that is how things looked at the beginning, then in the next fifty years the other kinds of materials now preeminent in our Talmud were added. If the original conception was to join Tosefta to the Mishnah, then the next program was to amplify and vastly augment discourse both concerning these compilations and also independent of them. These comments, however, should not be misunderstood to represent a thesis on the history of the formation of the Yerushalmi. They simply point to striking phenomena, apparent to the naked eye, so to speak, as soon as we differentiate among types of units of discourse and ask about how they are arranged.

I differentiate among six possible relationships to the Mishnah-pericope at hand, hence six types of units of discourse.

1. *Mishnah-Exegesis*: These units of discourse take up the systematic and direct exegesis of the Mishnah-pericopes. They normally are the very starting-point of the Talmud's discussion.

2. *Tosefta: Citation and Exegesis*: The Palestinian Talmud frequently cites verbatim, or nearly verbatim, statements that also are found in Tosefta. Where there are differences in wording between what we find in the Talmud and what we find in the Tosefta as we now have it, moreover, time and again we discover that the Talmud's discussion presupposes the text now found in Tosefta, rather than that now found in the Talmud. For that reason I do not think we claim too much in regarding this sort of material as Tosefta's contribution. I hasten to add the qualification that much more work has to be done on the matter. When Tosefta does appear, it tends to come up fairly early in the unfolding of the Talmud's discourse. In a fair number of instances in which there is no clearcut discourse on the Mishnah-passage itself, the Talmud will cite Tosefta and discuss that. The Talmud's contribution to the exegesis of the Mishnah often consists in the elucidation of Tosefta's complement to the Mishnah, an orderly procedure indeed. But this is a tendency, not a fixed rule.

3. *Legal Speculation and Reflection Primary to the Mishnah*: A unit of discourse may well carry forward a discussion superficially separate from the Mishnah. Yet upon routine inquiry, we notice that the discussion at hand speculates on principles introduced, to begin with, in the Mishnah's rule or in Tosefta's complement to that rule. These units of discourse tend to be more complex in a structure, commonly, also a good bit longer, than those of 1 and 2. There is a marked tendency for this type of unit to be included only in sequence after the first and second types.

4. *Harmonization of Distinct Laws of the Mishnah*: One of the most interesting units of discourse is that in which principles are abstracted from utterly unrelated rules of the Mishnah (less commonly: of Tosefta). These are then shown to intersect and to conflict; or opinions and principles of a given authority on one such matter will be shown to differ from those of that same authority on another, intersecting matter. These units tend to occur at several different tractates verbatim, since they serve equally well (or poorly) each Mishnah-pericope cited therein. Like those of category 3, these units of discourse vastly amplify the principles of the Mishnah. But they do not serve for a close exegesis of its wording or specific rule. These entries are few, but always substantial

and difficult, since several different kinds of law have to be mastered, then the underlying principles made explicit and brought into juxtaposition with those of other laws on other topics.

5. *Legal Speculation and Reflection Independent of the Passage of the Mishnah at Hand*: There are units of discourse essentially autonomous of the Mishnah-pericope with which they now are associated. These will pursue questions not even indirectly generated by the law in hand. From time to time we may guess at why the redactor thought the discourse belonged where he placed it. While there are not a great many of these, as in the foregoing instance, they are long and involved, and always difficult and unusually interesting. They tend to occur not at the initial stages of a Talmudic passage attached to a pericope of the Mishnah, but rather late in the sequence of types of units of discourse. At Baba Meṣia, for example, with its rather brief units of discourse, dominated by (mere) citation of Tosefta, they invariably occur in the second of two units. In Sanhedrin we find them at the higher end of the scale of numbers of units of discourse, and the same is so, in general, at Niddah and Sukkah. But this is only a tendency, by no means a rule so fixed as the one governing placement of units of discourse devoted to Mishnah-exegesis.

6. *Anthology, Relevant to the Mishnah only in Theme*: There are sizable units of discourse joined together only by a common theme, and joined to the Mishnah-pericope at which they occur only because, in some rather general way, someone supposed that their themes and the themes of the Mishnah intersect. This type of unit of discourse is especially common in tractate Sanhedrin, and, in particular, it predominates in those chapters at which the Mishnah's statements, for their part, pertain not to law but to lore. Most such anthologies are rich in collections of citation of and comment upon verses of Scripture. But in the present category are by no means the bulk of the Talmud's Scriptural exegesis and comments in the tractates at hand. There is a tendency for this type of unit of discourse to occur late in the unfolding of a Talmudic passage assigned to a given Mishnah-pericope, just as is the case in the foregoing.

These overall results are offered as a description of tendencies and general traits of the arrangement of diverse types of units of discourse in the Talmud of the Land of Israel.

If the original plan for the arrangement of units of discourse was to deal first with the Mishnah, then with the Tosefta, and, finally, with other matters pertinent to Tosefta, then the Babas would illustrate how the Talmud of the Land of Israel would have looked, had that plan prevailed without augmentation. But other kinds of materials entirely—as differentiated against the common base of relationship to the Mishnah—came into being. These materials found an ample home for themselves elsewhere, but—in general—not in the Caesarean tractates. If I had more confidence in the consistency of my own taxonomy as well as in my system of dividing

Talmudic passages into units of discourse, I should offer statistics to give some precision to these statements. But to allow for the variables of impression and subjectivity, I make them only as accounts of overall tendencies and probably-recurrent phenomena. For my present purpose, this mode of discourse is ample.

The redactional program of the men responsible for laying out the materials of Yerushalmi may now be described in simple terms. Most important, we see that there was such a program. There is nothing in random or lacking in a plan. That is clear because, within the differentiation of units of discourse I have defined, diverse types of units of discourse are not mixed together promiscuously. There is a pronounced tendency to move from close reading of the Mishnah and then Tosefta to more general inquiry into the principles of a Mishnah-passage and their interplay with those of some other, superficially unrelated passage, and, finally, to more general reflections on law not self-evidently related to the Mishnah-passage at hand or to anthologies intersecting only at a general topic. Now while that program may appear to be self-evident and logical, we must not assume there were no choices in how to lay things out. The program I have described exhibits sufficient variation to rule out the possibility that our Talmud's is the only, not to say the best, way of doing things. The case of Baba Meṣia, moreover, different in program as is that tractate from the others we probed, leaves no doubt about the matter: *Things are the way they are because people wanted them to be this way and not some other way.* We know that because the paramount traits of several hundred Talmudic passages devoted to units of the Mishnah are, if not everywhere uniform, then fairly constant and consistent.

It therefore follows that the redactors of our five tractates knew precisely how they wished to lay out whatever materials they drew together into the Talmud. Accordingly, the work of redaction was active and followed a plan and a program. Whether or not that work was done in a single generation is unclear. Following Lieberman, we must concur that fifty years prior to the formation of the Palestinian Talmud as we know it, the first Talmud, the one made in Caesarea, followed the program we have uncovered. It may have been that the redactors of the rest of the Talmud accepted the plan of the Caesarean authorities for the tractates they later undertook to bring into being. Perhaps there was a shared program among the various schools: "Since we are studying the Mishnah and Tosefta as our principal texts, we shall now lay out some permanent guidelines on how to read these texts and interpret and apply them." The one thing that is clear is that the redactors took full charge of the layout of whatever materials came to hand. They made significant decisions about the order in which diverse types of discourse were to be carried on: this, then that.

If therefore we now take as fact that the Talmud before us is the result of a generation, or a number of generations, of redaction, it is because we see the evidences of active participation in the formation of the document: a plan, a program. The contrary possibility, that this is just how things happened to come to hand, seems unlikely, given the disproportionate replication of a single (logical, self-evident) pattern. The second question flows from the first. If the redactors participated in the organization of units of discourse, did they also place their mark upon the formulation of those same units of discourse? It is to this question that we must now turn.

vi. *From Redaction to Formulation?*

The facts we have reviewed suggest a general uniformity from one tractate to the next in redaction processes, with the important exception of the Babas, the Talmud of Caesarea. Even there, strikingly, the differences between redactional policy from other (more "normal") tractates lie not in what is included, but in what is omitted only from the triplet of these tractates. Accordingly we are on firm ground in maintaining that we may speak of the Talmud as a whole, even though our sample is only five tractates. Overall, we need always allow for variation here and there. But systematic work on the whole Talmud clearly was done, since, as we have seen, the fundamental policy governing organization of materials is uniform for the tractates at hand. It follows that we may turn from redaction to formulation. Once more, will all due respect for variation and diversity, we seek gross and general traits, affecting the whole of the Talmud under study.

Since the close interplay between redaction and formulation constitutes the single firm result of the study of the Mishnah, at the outset we ask about the same matter for our Talmud. The issue is whether we can find evidence of systematic attention to formulating units of discourse in such a way as to relate one to the next within a redactional program or process. If there is such evidence, we must conclude that even in the redactional stages of the formation of the Talmud, work went on not merely in minor correction, revision, or glossing of a passage, but even in the very formulation of the statement of its main points, in the wording, structure and form by which those points would be expressed. It would then follow that, on grounds of literary traits prior to the redaction of the whole, we are unable to posit the existence of units of discourse as we now know them. If we find no points of correlation between redactional policies and problems of formulation of units of discourse, it must follow that prior to the redactional stages (though we do not know how long before) a process of formulation of units of discourse was underway.

The upshot then is simple. Our question is this: Did the redactors work with essentially finished units of discourse? Did they themselves participate in the formation of the completed units of discourse which they also organized and laid side by side? The criterion for positive evidence for the second proposition—hence, also, negative evidence for the first—derives from comparison to the Mishnah. We compare units of discourse of our Talmud to the formulary traits of Mishnah-pericopes, seeing how they indicate the hand of redaction and organization within the very phrasing of individual units of law of this Mishnah. That is, we shall see that for the Mishnah essential to the organization and layout of completed units of discourse is the very pattern of formulating those same units of discourse. The result, as I have said, is proof for the Mishnah that redaction is prior, and critical, to formulation. Redaction is not solely a process of joining together statements bearing no formal relationship to one another, hence available prior (we do not know how long before) to the process of organization and layout we call redaction. A clear grasp of how the Mishnah works is then essential to a comparative inquiry into the Talmud's traits. Absence of equivalent traits then will signify a different relationship, for our Talmud, of redaction to formulation from that prevalent in the Mishnah.

The principal result of my inquiry into formulation and redaction in the Mishnah was to show constant and close relationship between the one and the other. Specifically, I found that when the Mishnah's redactors wished to indicate the formation of a unit of discourse (which I called, in that setting, "intermediate unit"), they would take up a distinctive formulary pattern or form different from that they had used beforehand and also from that they would use in the following unit. They would carefully group their smallest whole statements ("smallest units of cognition") so that each one would repeat the same syntactic pattern, setting up (in general) groups of three or multiples of three, or groups of five or multiples of five, with such internally patterned statements of a single principle being applied to a single theme. This seemed to me definitive evidence that the whole could not have been formulated prior to the work of redaction, at which point—and only at which point—the larger program of arrangement of topics and principles expressed in connection with said topics was in hand. Only when the whole was fully in view was it possible to form the parts in the way in which they were formed. There is no other economical way of explaining the facts I discovered since, as is clear, the whole was planned before the parts were laid out in their uniform and distinctive syntactic patterns and in their little sets of three or five repetitions of such patterns.

The issue when we turn to the Talmud of course cannot be framed in the same way. But to begin with, we must ask ourselves whether we discern any formulary patterns at all, not only of a redactional type. When we speak of formulary patterns, once again we mean recurrent arrangements of words in a give syntactic formula. Whether or not we may relate the use of such a pattern to a redactional plan is only second in line of inquiry. To present this matter as clearly as I can, I wish first of all to show, on two chapters selected more or less at random, the Mishnah's formal traits, and then, for those same chapters, look at those of the Talmud. The former and not the latter exhibit patterned language at a gross and recurrent level. I do not seek evidence from the recurrence of particles or rhetoric lacking more than merely conventional status in the formation of thought, that is, in deep syntactic structures. These merely rhetorical conventions have no standing whatsoever for the problem at hand. The fact that the speech of the document contains fixed rhetorical patterns signifies matters quite separate from the presence of patterns at the deep syntax of the document. The presence or absence of those other patterns of language, as distinct from mere rhetoric, alone testifies to the issue at hand. The fact, for example, that a Mishnah-passage will ordinarily be introduced with a rhetorical pattern, "We have learned there . . . ," does not seem to me to contain implications about the formulation of the construction in which the particles or rhetorical usages occur. They testify rather about the overall rhetorical conventions, independent of all context, of rabbinic discourse in general. In the nature of our inquiry, it is distinctive context that concerns us.

It is easier to prove than to disprove the proposition that a unit of discourse is framed to follow a syntactic pattern. In the former case I simply point out the traits of the pattern and then list all of the examples of that pattern. If I maintain, as I do, that the whole of the document is patterned, I further distinguish that pattern from some other and indicate the interrelationships and proportions of each in the whole. Should there be (to my eye) unpatterned units, I so indicate. I also am able to point to the limits of the formalization of syntax and formulations. This I do by showing those parts of a unit of discourse—as distinct from those whole units of discourse—in which I discern no distinctive formulations or recurrent patterns at all. But wishing to show the *independence* of formulation from redaction, how am I supposed to prove that a unit of discourse follows *no* syntactic pattern? A catalogue of non-patterned instances must include all possible examples. That is hardly worth the effort. To show the points of formalization, in contrast to the earlier exercise, matters are still less self-explanatory.

Accordingly, the simplest strategy to make the basic point at hand is to present two instances in which redaction plays a role in the patterned formulation of a sizable unit of discourse, then to present the Talmud's contribution to the same unit of discourse. This allows us to contrast the Mishnah's with the Talmud's gross literary traits. We shall then see what a passage looks like when redaction controls formulation—selection of recurrent forms and formulary patterns—and so recognize what a passage looks like when it does not. While two striking examples hardly prove anything, the reader is then able to make a survey of any number of Mishnah-passages, chapters, or even whole tractates. The same result will be replicated at most points. While, in due course, we may find forms of consequence in our Talmud, we shall invariably find them wholly out of phase with any redactional purpose discernible to us.

We proceed to deal with one unit of Baba Meṣia, because here the Talmud of the Land of Israel is brief and highly disciplined. Then we consider one of Sanhedrin. Accordingly, if we are going to find formalization of the Talmud's units of discourse, it is more likely to be in the context of a Caesarean tractate than a later one, hence using both an earlier and a later tractate is advisable. The latter tractate bears heavy accretions of all sorts, beyond the modest limits of Mishnah-exegesis, Tosefta-citation and exegesis. Accordingly, we look first to the most likely source for examples of some sort of patterning based on redactional considerations—agglomeration of units—of the formulation of the language of the Talmud. We should find ourselves more adequately situated if we could find at least a few examples of what, in the Mishnah, we locate everywhere. The fact is that I can find not a single instance, in the twenty-nine tractates I have translated, in which the unit of discourse is so formulated as to indicate an intention to relate what is formulated to its redactional context or to the larger needs of putting together two or more completed units of thought into a redactional unit (a complete discussion of a Mishnah-pericope, for instance). Let us now briefly review our passages.

First we deal with the Mishnah-pericope, given in italics, as a unit, then with the accompanying Talmudic discussion of it. While the division of the Talmud breaks up what in fact are formal units, the fact need not concern us, since it is not primary to the text but the work of copyists and even printers. A brief comment at the end of the Mishnah-passage is intended to highlight the formal traits, unifying several distinct statements into a single, patterned whole, and this without regard to the time in which authorities cited in the passage were believed to have flourished, let alone traits of speech characteristic of individual authorities. Then the Talmudic discussion of that Mishnah-passage, viewed as a whole, is reproduced. Where the Talmud breaks up a Mishnah-unit into two parts (or more), I have preserved my original unit-numbering system, so indicated here; this facilitates reference to the translation. A Roman numeral at the side of a Mishnah-unit signifies one component of a whole unit of tradition, matched in its patterned language, as I explain, with other such units, also indicated by Roman numbers. The final number then indicates the number of examples of each formal entry in the whole construction.

Mishnah Baba Meṣia 1:1-2

I.
- A. *Two [in court] lay hold of a cloak—*
- B. *This one says, "I found it!"—*
- C. *And that one says, "I found it!"—*
- D. *This one says, "It's all mine!"—*
- E. *And that one says, "It's all mine!"—*
- F. *This one takes an oath that he has no less a share of it than half,*
- G. *and that one takes an oath that he has no less a share of it than half.*
- H. *And they divide it up.*

II.
- I. *This one says, "It's all mine!"*
- J. *And that one says, "Half of it is mine!"*
- K. *The one who says, "It's all mine," takes an oath that he has no less a share of it than three parts.*
- L. *And the one who says, "Half if it is mine," takes an oath that he has no less a share of it than a fourth part.*
- M. *This one then takes three shares, and that one takes the fourth.*

M.B.M. 1:1

III.
- A. *Two were riding on a beast,*
- B. *or one was riding and one was leading it—*
- C. *This one says, "It's all mine!"—*
- D. *and that one says, "It's all mine!"—*
- E. *this one takes an oath that he has no less a share of it than half,*
- F. *and that one takes an oath that he has no less a share of it than half.*
- G. *And they divide it.*
- H. *But when they concede [that they found it together] or have witnesses to prove it, they divide it without taking an oath.*

M.B.M. 1:2

The recurrent triplicate-pattern is not in the first clause of the apocapated sentence, that is, M. 1:1A, 1:2A, B, but rather in the second, that is M. 1:1B-E, I-J, M. 1:2C-D. The repeated triplicate-pattern in the apodosis of the same sentence, M. 1:1F-G, H, M. 1:1K-M, and M. 1:2E-G, is not to be missed. So what we have are three individual statements, all of them constructed in extreme apocopation, illustrative of three aspects of the same point. The several statements may or may not represent diverse authorities' views. They may or may not have existed in some prior, and different form. We only know that, in order to put together the several ideas before us, expressive of several aspects of the same general conception, the framer of the whole also participated in the formulation of the individual components. Otherwise we should not likely see the recurrent syntactic patterns that are before us. Hence redaction plays a principal role governing the character of formulation of the pericope, and that is without regard to what is stated in the laws themselves. We proceed now to the Talmud, which treats M. 1:1 separate from M. 1:2.

Y. Baba Meṣia 1:1

I. A. [The following is a paraphrase of Tosefta Shebuot 5:3, which is as follows: If the plaintiff was claiming a *maneh* in the presence of a court, and the defendant denied it, and two witnesses came and gave testimony that he owes him fifty *zuz*, lo, this one pays (fifty *zuz*) and is exempt from the requirement of taking an oath. But if there was only a single witness who was giving evidence against him, lo, this one takes an oath covering the whole amount.] It was taught: A man who said to his fellow, "Give me the *maneh* which you owe me!"

B. The other said to him, "It never happened!"

C. The lender went and brought witnesses that he owes him fifty *zuz*. . . .

D. [Concerning the foregoing case,] R. Hiyya the Elder said, "The admission by witnesses [that the man owes the money] is tantamount to his own admission [that he owes part of the debt, namely, the fifty *zuz* which the witnesses say has been lent out of the hundred claimed by the creditor],

E. "and consequently, the borrower must take an oath covering the remainder [of what has been claimed by the creditor]."

F. R. Yohanan said, "The admission by witnesses is by no means tantamount to his own admission which would produce the consequence that the borrower must take an oath covering the remainder [and he need not do so]."

G. Said R. L, "The position of R. Hiyya the Great derives from: *Two in court lay hold of a cloak* [M. B.M. 1:1A–H]. Since the man is holding on to half of [the cloak], it is as if he brought witnesses to court that half of it belongs to him. And you then rule that he takes an oath [as at M. 1:1F, G] and retains possession of the half in his hand.

"Now this case before us is similar to that case. [Possession of the cloak is deemed parallel to having witnesses to ownership thereof.]"

II. A. Rabbah bar Mamal and R. Amram introduced the following issue of Rab into [the present discussion]:

B. [Rab] said to [R. Hiyya], "Do they then not hand over an oath [for swearing by] someone suspect of lying? [For the debtor of T. Shebu. 5:3, cited above, has alleged that he owes nothing. The witnesses prove that he is a liar. How then can he take an oath covering the remainder since he is a known perjurer?]."

C. He said to him, "Even a statement using the language of an oath [but omitting the operative clauses] they do not hand over to him."

III. A. [With reference to M. 1:1F, G: *This one takes an oath that he has no less a share of it than half . . . ,*] how does he then swear? [What sort of language is used here? For the claim is that the man owns not less than half of the cloak. Even if the man owns none of the cloak, he can make that statement without in fact lying under oath, since, indeed, he does not own less than half, for he owns none of it.]

B. R. Huna said, "'By an oath! I have a right to it, and I own no less of it than part worth a *perutah.*' [By using this language, the problem of A is avoided. These are meaningful statements.]"

IV. A. [Reverting to I G,] said R. Yohanan, "If from this matter [that the parallel to M. B.M. 1:1 is decisive], [you prove that an oath is required], then it is an oath [at M. B.M. 1:1] which has been ordained as a remedy [by the rabbis]. [Each party may take that same oath and further the two parties could divide the claimed cloak without taking any oath at all insofar as their actual possession is the equivalent of witnesses to their claim. Accordingly, the case of M. B.M. 1:1 is not pertinent to the matter under discussion at T. Shebu. 5:3 at all, with the consequence that the claim of Rabbi La is not valid.]"

V. A. It was taught: <u>Two who were laying hold of a document</u> [bond]—

B. <u>This one says, "It is mine, and I lost it!"</u>

C. <u>And that one says, "It was in my possession, and I already paid you for it!"</u>—

D. <u>"Let the document be confirmed through the signatures of the witnesses which it bears," the words of Rabbi.</u>

E. <u>And (Rabban Simeon b.) Gamaliel says, "Let them divide it</u> [the <u>money] between them]"</u> [T. B.M. 1:15]. [Rabbi's position is that the former admits that he has written the bond and it is necessary to confirm the bond. If the creditor is able to do so, he has a valid claim and divides up the money covered by the bond. If not, the creditor has no share in the proceeds of the bond. Simeon b. Gamaliel's position is that it is not necessary even to confirm the bond; in any event the claimants divide the funds at issue.]

F. R. Eleazar said, "All follows the circumstance of which of the claimants holds the part on which the witnesses have signed their names. [The party holding the part of the bond containing the confirmation by witnesses is the one who wins the case.]"

G. Said R. Hisda, "If you accept this view, you accord with the position of R. Simeon [b. Gamaliel]. [But Rabbi will want the witnesses to confirm the bond in court.]"

VI. A. This one says, "It's all mine!"
B. And that one says, "A third of it is mine!"
C. The one who says, "It's all mine," takes an oath that he has no less of a share of it than five parts.
D. And the one who says, "A third of it is mine!" takes an oath that he has no less of a share of it than a sixth [part].
E. The governing principle of the matter: One is subjected to an oath only up to one-half of his claimed share alone [T. B.M. 1:2].

If each claims the whole thing, then it is divided. But the one who claims only half concedes to the other party the other half, in which case we divide only the half under dispute. So the claimant of the half takes a fourth, and the claimant of the whole takes the half conceded by the other as well as the quarter he gains in the compromise. The Talmud presents a fairly well sustained and varied discussion of M.'s pericope. The obvious question to someone who knows the Mishnah will be the relationship between the oath of which M. B.M. 1:1 speaks and the larger theory of oaths at tractate Shebuot. This is what is accomplished at units I, II, and IV, interrupted by the brief interpolation at unit III. The discussion is formally disjointed but subtantively coherent. Units V and VI then move on, quite systematically, to important ideas of Tosefta, with the former analyzed, the latter simply cited for information. This brings us to the Talmud for M. B.M. 1:2.

Y. Baba Meṣia 1:2

I. A. Said R. Huna, "There it is taught:
B. "A woman who was riding along on a beast, with two men leading it,
C. "[and she comes to court and claims,] 'These are my slaves, and the ass and its burden belong to me,'
D. "While this one says, 'This is my wife, and the other man is my slave, and the ass and its burden are mine,'
E. "and the other party claims, 'this is my wife, and the other man is my slave, and the ass and its burden are mine'—
F. "she requires a writ of divorce from each of the men, and she must also declare both of them free men.

G. "And both of them issue writs of emancipation to one another.

H. "And as to the ass and its burden, all three of them lay an equal claim [and divide it up]."

The inescapable conclusion is that the considerations important in the formulation of the Mishnah-passage play no role whatsoever in the framing of the Talmud's units of discourse, jointly or severally. As a group, of course, there is not a single stylistic trait in common. Individually, the units appear discrete from one another. Unit I provides a set of declarative sentences, in which several rabbis comment on a case supplied, essentially, out of Tosefta. Unit II follows the same pattern, a kind of artificial debate-discourse, in which the sole recurrent formulation consists in the attributive particle (said, or, he said to him). This adds up to nothing, since the substance of what is said is unaffected. Units III and IV have in common an uncited allusion to a phrase of the Mishnah. Beyond that point there is no trace of formalized syntax. The same pattern we see at unit I—allusion to, or citation of, Tosefta—recurs at the end. All is consistent in relating to the Mishnah. The organization clearly is dictated by the sequence of clauses—details—of the Mishnah-passage. But there is not the slightest indication that the formulation of the passages aimed at formalized patterning of the language for any purpose whatever. The Talmud serving M. B.M. 1:2 consists simply of a statement of Huna, citing some antecedent corpus. The Talmud's case is simply a variation on the Mishnah's. One may see at y. B.M. 1:2C, D, E, and F, G, H, some sort of imitation of the speech-patterns of the Mishnah. For our purposes that fact changes nothing.

Since it may fairly be claimed that this one of the tractates of Caesarea bears special traits and is unrepresentative of the generality of the Talmud of the Land of Israel, we turn, for our second exercise, to tractate Sanhedrin. Further, we choose a Mishnah-passage in which the pattern of syntax is simpler and more directly accessible: five instances of a single kind of declarative-sentence, followed by a separate but related rule.

Mishnah Sanhedrin 1:3

I. A. *They judge a tribe, a false prophet [Deut 18:20], and a high priest, only on the instructions of a court of seventy-one members.*

II. B. *They bring forth [the army] to wage an optional war only on the instructions of a court of seventy-one.*

III. C. *They make additions to the city [of Jerusalem] and to the courtyards [of the Temple] only on the instructions of a court of seventy-one.*

IV. D. *They set up sanhedrins for the tribes only on the instructions of a court of seventy-one.*

V. E. *They declare a city to be "an apostate city" [Deut 13:12ff.]*

only on the instructions of a court of seventy-one.
F. *And they do not declare a city to be "an apostate city" on the frontier,*
G. *[nor do they declare] three [in one locale] to be apostate cities,*
H. *but they do so in the case of one or two.*

Y. Sanhedrin 1:3

I. A. One should take note of the following: two individuals [namely, the false prophet and the high priest] are not judged [by an ordinary court]. It is not an argument *a fortiori* that an entire tribe [should not be judged by an ordinary court, but only by one of seventy-one members]?
   B. Said R. Mattenaiah, "The Mishnah-pericope refers to the patriarch of a tribe [and not a whole tribe, for that is an obvious fact]. [The point is that the patriarch of a tribe is judged only by a sanhedrin with seventy-one members.]"
   C. Said R. Eliezer, "The Mishnah speaks of a tract of forest between the territory of two tribes [and makes the point that, if there is a suit involving such territory, then even though it is a property case, it is settled by a court of seventy-one, just as, to begin with, the Land was divided up in accord with the instructions of such a court]."

II. A. Said R. Zira, "'Presumptuously' ['The man who acts presumptuously, but not obeying the priest . . . shall die' (Deut 17:12)] is stated in one context, and 'presumptuously' ['But the prophet who presumes to speak a word in my name which I have not commanded him to speak, . . . the prophet has spoken it presumptuously . . .' (Deut 18:20,22)] is stated in another context.
   B. "Just as in the reference to presumptuousness in the latter passage Scripture speaks of a false prophet, so in the reference to presumptuousness in the former passage, Scripture speaks of a false prophet."
   C. Said R. Hezekiah, "'Speaking' is mentioned in the one context ['According to the instructions which they give you, and according to the decision which they pronounce to you, you shall do' (Deut 17:11)], and later on it is stated, '. . . when a prophet speaks in the name of the Lord . . .' (Deut 18:22).
   D. "Just as in the latter usage Scripture speaks of a false prophet, so in the former instance, the same usage indicates that Scripture speaks of a false prophet."

III. A. *They bring forth the army to wage an optional war only on the instructions of a court of seventy-one* [M. San. 1:3B]. *[They make additions to the city . . . only on the instruction of a* court of seventy-one (M. San. 1:3C).] [The following serves M. Shebu. 2:2B-F: *They add to the city and courtyards only on the instructions of the king and prophet, the Urim and Thummin, and the Sanhedrin of seventy-one members, with two thank offerings and singing. The court goes along with the two thank offerings behind them, and all the Israelites after them. The one offered inside is eaten, and the one offered outside is burned. And any area which is not treated wholly in this way (with the proper rites)—he who enters that area—they are not liable on that account.*]

B. R. Judah says, "At the outset [of designating the holy ground of Jerusalem], 'So David went up at God's word' (2 Sam 24:19)—thus the king and prophet [of M. Shebu. 2:2].

C. "'Then Solomon began to build the house of the Lord in Jerusalem on Mount Moriah, where the Lord had appeared [to David his father]' (2 Chr 3:1)—thus the Urim and Thummim.

D. "'To David, his father'—this refers to the Sanhedrin.

E. "'Ask your father, and he will show you, your elders, and they will tell you' (Deut 32:7)—[this refers to consecrating the new territory] with song.

F. "'And after them went Hoshaiah and half of the princes of Judah' (Neh 12:32)—[this refers to the requirement of bringing] thank offerings."

G. "And I appointed two great companies which gave thanks and went in procession. One went to the right upon the wall to the Dung Gate" (Neh 12:31).

H. Said R. Samuel bar Yudan, "Why is it written, 'moved in procession,' not 'walked in procession'? The meaning is that the thank offerings were carried by another person [and did not go on foot]."

I. R. Huna bar Hiyya in the name of Rab derived from the Torah itself [proof that the king, prophet, Urim and Thummim, and Sanhedrin, are required to add to the city]: "According to all that I show you concerning the pattern of the tabernacle, and of all its furniture, so you shall make it" (Exod 25:9).

J. "Thus you shall make it"—for generations to come.

K. "Moses stands for the king and prophet.

L. "And Aaron stands for the Urim and Thummim.

M. "'And the Lord said to Moses, Gather for me seventy men of the elders of Israel' (Num 11:16)—this refers to the Sanhedrin.

N. "'Ask your father and he will show you, your elders, and they will tell you' (Deut 32:7)—[this refers to consecrating the new territory] with song.

O. "'And after them went Hoshaiah and half of the princes of

Judah' (Neh 12:32)—[this refers to the requirement of bringing] thank offerings.

P. "'And I appointed two great companies which gave thanks and went in procession. One went to the right upon the wall to the Dung Gate' (Neh. 12:31)."

Q. Said R. Samuel bar Yudan, "Why is it written, 'moved in procession' and not, 'walked in procession'? The meaning is that the thank offerings were carried by another person [and did not go on foot]."

R. How were they borne?

S. R. Hiyya the Great and R. Simeon bar Rabbi—one said, "One opposite the other," and the other said, "One behind another."

T. Both of them interpret biblical verse: "The other company of those who gave thanks went to the left, and I followed them" (Neh 12:38).

U. The one who says they came opposite one another [cites as evidence]: "They are dwelling opposite me" (Num 22:5).

V. The one who says they came one after another [cites as evidence]: "He shall wring its head from behind its neck" (Lev 5:8).

W. The one who says that they came toward one another maintains that it so happened that every place was atoned for with a single thank offering.

X. The one who said, they came one after the other maintains that it turned out that every place was atoned for through two thank offerings.

Y. The one who maintains that they came one after the other finds no difficulty in that which we have learned: the inner one [nearest the court] is eaten, and the outer one is burned [T. San. 3:4E].

Z. But the one who maintains that they came toward one another—which of the two thank offerings will be the inner one?

AA. It is the one which is nearer to the house [the Temple].

BB. R. Yosa in the name of R. Yohanan: "At the instruction of a prophet is the thank offering [offered on the occasion of the consecration of the city] to be eaten."

CC. Said R. Zira, "There we learn: 'If the prophet is here, then what need have I for the Urim and Thummim?'"

DD. He found it taught: R. Judah says, "There is need for Urim and Thummim."

IV. A. Said R. Abbahu, "R. Yohanan and R. Simeon b. Laquish differed.

B. "One said, 'First they build, then they consecrate.'

C. "The other said, 'First they consecrate, then they build.'"

D. As to the view of him who said, "First they build and then they consecrate"—do they not regard the walls [of the Temple] as if they were burnt offerings [so how will it be possible to continue the building process once the Temple has been consecrated]?

V. A. [If] they wished to add to the courtyards, with what [offerings] do they [commemorate] the additions?
B. With two loaves of [leavened] bread.
C. And do they consecrate [Temple-space] on a festival day? [Where will they get leavened bread?]
D. But: it is done with the show bread [after it is removed from the altar].
E. And do they consecrate on the Sabbath [when that bread is put out]?
F. But: it is done by night.
G. But do they consecrate by night?
H. Said R. Yose b. R. Bun, "[They consecrate] with a meal offering which is baked in the oven [which may be eaten in the courtyard]."
I. This view is suitable for the case in which they came up from the Exile, in which case they made an offering, and afterward they consecrated the Temple.
J. But when they entered the Land, how did they consecrate?
K. Said R. Yose b. R. Bun, "With two thank offerings which come from Nob and Gibeon."

VI. A. Abba Saul says, "There were two valleys in Jerusalem, a lower one and an upper one.
B. "The lower one was sanctified with all these procedures, but the upper one was not sanctified.
C. "And when the Exiles came up, without a king, without Urim, without Thummim, in the lower one, which had been consecrated completely, the people of the land would eat Lesser Holy Things and second tithe, and associates would eat Lesser Holy Things but not second tithe.
D. "And in the upper one, which had not been consecrated completely, the people of the land would eat Lesser Holy Things and not second tithe, while the associates [would eat] neither Lesser Holy Things nor a second tithe.
E. "And on what account did they not sanctify it? Because it was a weak point in Jerusalem, and was easily conquered" [T. San. 3:4].

VII. A. *They set up sanhedrins for the tribes only [on the instructions of a court of seventy-one]* (M. San. 1:3D).
B. Scripture says, "[You shall appoint judges and officers in all your towns which the Lord your God gives you, according] to your

VIII. A. *They declare a city to be an apostate city*, ect. (M. San. 1:3E–H).
　B. R. Yohanan in the name of R. Hoshaiah: "There are three authorities [who differ in this regard].
　C. "One said, 'One they do declare to be apostate, two they do not declare to be apostate' (cf. M. San. 1:3F–H).
　D. "Another said, 'Those that are contiguous they declare apostate cities, those that are scattered about they do not declare apostate cities.'
　E. "And the third said, 'Those that are scattered they do not declare apostate cities at all, lest gentiles break in and enter the Land of Israel.'"
　F. [18c] And there is he who proposes to state, "Lest the enemy break in and come upon totally unsettled areas [meeting no resistance because of the absence of population]."

Following two rather routine exercises, units I, II, the Talmud concentrates its attention on M. 1:3C. But here the point of interest is not the pericope before us, but, rather, M. Shebu., 2:2, as cited. Clearly, III E–H, N–Q, require attention. It seems to me that S carries forward N–Q, E–H break into the discourse established by A–D, I–M, so it is the former appearance which must be deleted. Units IV, V, and VI enrich the discussion of consecrating Jerusalem and the Temple area; here too the appropriate pericope is at M. Shebuot. So we are left with I, II, and, at the end, VII, VIII, all of them brief and essentially descriptive pericopae.

The foregoing comment leaves no doubt that before us is a miscellany. The stylistic side to things clearly indicates no one was concerned to formalize language or to establish any sort of encompassing structural, let alone syntactic, patterns at all. There are conventions operative in the formation of some materials (sometimes awkwardly translated by me, e.g., IA, "One should take note . . ."). Once more we notice ample use of the attributive particle, which proves nothing. There is a form of a dispute at IIIS: "Name I, Name II, one said . . . and the other said . . ." Such a construction bears no redactional implications that I can discern. The formalization that follows, "Both of them . . . , the one who says . . . , the one who says . . . , the one who said . . . , the one who said . . . , and so on," is striking, and the whole may be important. But it is unrelated to the larger arrangement of the materials of which it is part. We may say, therefore, that IIIS–AA exhibits important formalized traits affecting its own formulation—that is, the way that sub-unit itself is expressed. But these formal traits have no bearing upon its location among other, distinct sub-units of discourse. That is clear when we reach unit IV, and find the same formal construction. There is no way that one can argue unit IV has been placed where it is, or formulated the way it is, because of its proximity or other relationship to IIIS-AA. The other units or parts of units seems to me lacking in any striking evidences of patterning of languages or recurrent syntactic patterns of any sort.

vii. Conclusion

These exercises suffice to illustrate a simple proposition. If the traits of the Mishnah indicate that central to the process of organizing materials was the work of formulating them, then the absence of the same traits in the Talmud indicates the opposite. The work of redaction of units of discourse in the Talmud therefore was distinct from, and later than, the work of formulation. There was a distinct stage of redaction, in which already available materials were laid out in accord with a few simple rules, governed by the relationship to the Mishnah exhibited by a given unit of discourse.

We now have a notion of what the two documents look like when seen whole and complete, hence also in contrast to one another. It is banal to note that much more work needs to be done. To begin to describe the Talmud of the Land of Israel as a whole, I have investigated its gross redactional traits, on the one side, and ask about the impact, if any, of redaction upon the formulation of the several units of discourse of which the Talmud is composed, on the other. We can now describe how the redactors did their work and what they proposed to accomplish. We also know that they worked with essentially finished units of discourse. These they shaped into extended discussions focused upon the passages of the Mishnah, in sequence. So the Talmud is made to appear to carry forward and amplify what is in the Mishnah.

In point of fact the Talmud viewed at the end does considerably more than that. For the system of thought revealed by Yerushalmi and that constructed by the Mishnah, despite the interplay of superficial detail, are essentially different from one another. The Mishnah's system presents issues important to the surviving priesthood of the second century in rhetoric precious to the surviving scribes of that same time. It knows nothing of rabbis and their authority, exegesis of Torah as the basis of law, schools as the foci of Jewish authority, and all of the other distinctive and characteristic traits of Judaism as expressed by the Talmud of the Land of Israel (all the more so, the other Talmud as well). So the substance of the Talmud bears witness against its redactional form. But that is a separate question, to be investigated in its own framework.

www.ingramcontent.com/pod-product-compliance
Lightning Source LLC
Chambersburg PA
CBHW072153160426
43197CB00012B/2369